A Century of Hope

A Century of Hope

By

Jake C. Miller

ISBN: 1-58820-700-5 (e-book)
ISBN: 1-58820-701-3 (Paperback)

This book printed on acid free paper.

1stBooks - rev. 02/26/03

Jake C. Miller

A Century of Hope

With the 20th Century came many technological advancements and accompanying these changes were what appeared to be problems which did not lend themselves to solutions. For those of us who thought that we had seen the best of everything during that century, this new one is expected to be one of breakthrough after breakthrough. We welcome the 21st Century as the *Century of Hope*. This collection of poetry challenges us to be innovative in order to prevent it from fading into a century of disillusionment.

Some of the writings in this book are found in other collections by the author including, "Everyone's a Teacher in *Building A Better World,* Daytona Beach, Florida, Pearce Publishers, 1996; "Constitutional Rights of Blacks," and "Millions on the March," in *In Search of A Better Day*, and "Bearers of Our Dreams," and "Flowers Not Weeds," in *Childhood to Adulthood.*

A Century of Hope

Table of Contents

A Beautiful World 1
A Commitment to Humanity 2
Accepting Responsibilities 3
An Instrument of Social Justice 4
Another Time and Place 5
Bearers of Our Dreams 6
Before This Day is Done 7
Beginning of a New Century 8
Bridging the Gap 9
Champion of a Cause 10
Changing Society 11
Choosing Our Causes 12
Commitment to Service......... 13
Constitutional Rights of Blacks 13
Diminishing the Violence...... 14
Directions 15
Diversity in a Pluralistic Society 16
Education.............................. 17
End of a Century 18
Entering the 21st Century...... 19
Environmental Concerns 20
Everyone's a Teacher............ 21
Exclude None 22
Falling Apart 23
Filling the Vacuum............... 24
Flow of Creative Ideas 25
Flowers Not Weeds 26
Freedom to Discuss 27
From the Sea Shore..........28
Gatekeepers 29
Global is Our Community30
Heed the Cry of the Needy 31
Honesty as Our Trademark 32
In Anticipation.................33
In Charge of My Destiny .34
In Search of Peace 35
In Search of Racial Understanding 36
Innovation........................36
Judging of Others............37
Lending a Helping Hand..38
Making an Impact...........39
Making Democracy a Reality 40
Measures of Adulthood ...42
Menaces to Society 42
Millions on the March 44
Morning 45
My Spoken Words 46
Obstacle in My Own Way Standing........................46
Obtaining Respect............47
Opportunity......................48
Our Failures 49
Our Heroes and Heroines.50
Our Homeland 51
Our Struggle Against Drug Abuse 52
Our World of Tomorrow .53

Parents in Search for Success 54
Passing the Torch 56
Prepare for the Transition...... 57
Preserver of the Peace 57
Prevailing Winds of Peace 58
Reacting to Raging Storms.... 60
Reality 60
Reawakening 61
Reliance on Government 62
Restraining the Oppressors.... 63
Retreat Not from Progress..... 64
Road to Somewhere.............. 65
Roles of Tradition.................. 66
Scars of the Past 67
Search for Solutions 68
Secure at Home?.................... 68
Selfish Pursuits...................... 69
Show Me Evidence................ 70
Solid Foundation 71
Solutions are Within Our Reach.................................. 72
Spending a Day With Children.............................. 73
Swimming Upstream............. 74
Teamwork.............................. 75
These Houses are Not Homes 75
Tomorrow is an Extension of Today 76
Understudies.......................... 78
Uniting Our Efforts for Peace 78
Utilize Potentials 80
Values We Instill.................... 81
Ventures 81
Very Few Possessions 82
Violence...........................83
Voices 84
Volunteerism 85
When Your Word is Given 86
Where the Wind Blows....86
Why 88
Why the Alienation..........88
With Our Riches 90
Xenophobia......................90
Yesterdays of My Life.....91
Youths in an Age of Confusion 92
Bridges............................94
Courage as a Weapon 95
Feeling Rewarded............96
Freedom 97
Humanitarians..................98
Impact 99
Influencing the Future ...100
Integrity 101
New Life for the Nation.101
Racism 103
Seize the Opportunity 103
Time to Awake 104
The Past is With Us 105

A Beautiful World

I want to paint a picture of a beautiful world,
where human-caused suffering exists no more.
A picture which depicts us at our very best,
as in harmony with nature and in peace we live.
Where weapons of war spoil not the landscape;
where pollution clouds not the heavenly skies;
where no trace of starvation in the picture appears,
and homeless people now in houses reside.
I want to compose music about a beautiful world--
a world of which so long I have dreamed;
compose music for people who dance with glee
to reflect the happiness which now they feel;
compose marches, not for war, but in celebration
of the peace which then will encompass the world;
compose songs for children joyfully to sing,
because fear and suffering they know no more.
I want to write a poem about a beautiful world--
a world where hatred has come to an end;
a world in which no one lives in fear,
for violence around us will be a thing of the past;
a world in which by united efforts,
complicated problems we would have resolved;
A poem I will write about that victorious day,
when the world of beauty came into play.
For long, I have dreamed of a beautiful world,
where beautiful people dominate the scene.
Beautiful thoughts they constantly think,
and beautiful deeds they usually do.
Beautiful people are great attractions,
because they bring beauty to any cause.
Therefore, all people should display their beauty,
so we can live is a beautiful world.

A Commitment to Humanity

To humanity I have a commitment,
which I am obligated to fulfill.
Both goods and services I must render,
to enhance the building of a better world.
An investment I have in humankind,
since my well-being on it depends.
An obligation I accept to promote its cause,
for when it advances, it elevates me.
All of humanity is my concern,
not only persons of my race, class and creed.
By actions of others I am affected
since each strengthens or weakens me.
My burdens are shared by those who are stronger,
and I share the load of those who are weak.
I am brought to tears when others suffer,
and with those who are happy I am full of glee.
Sometimes alone I can employ my talents,
the cause of humankind to assist.
Also at times I must work with others
since through cooperation we can better exist.
Extensive progress during the last century we made,
but greater is the work which remains to be done.
Humanity requires our foremost efforts;
therefore, there is a task for everyone.
Uneven has been the rewards of society,
causing the masses in misery to live.
The last century has had its complicated problems,
which to this one it will certainly give.
So anxiously we awaited the 21st Century,
with the many innovations which surely will come.
The fruits of new efforts we anticipate enjoying,
but its pains and suffering we must also endure.
Because with talents we are truly gifted;
there is much we can give to enhance humankind.

Therefore, each of us must respond to the challenge
as we come to terms with the century of hope.
From the fruits of society. I have freely partaken
some of the best which it had to give.
Therefore, a commitment to humanity I make,
and honor it I will to the best I can.

Accepting Responsibilities

For each action I take there are consequences.
Of this I am fully aware.
Therefore, for each act I choose to take,
there are responsibilities which I must willingly bear.
If the results of my actions are commendable,
the credit will be attributed to me.
If however, my actions result in failure,
then, from the blame I shall never be free.
If an effective person I am ever to become,
realistic must be my appraisal of me.
I must recognize that life consists of successes and failures,
and with both I must be able to cope.
Graciously, I should accept praise when I have succeeded,
and acknowledge defeat without placing blame.
What do I gain by giving excuses for failure,
when the truth I know all too well?
Do I give the impression that I am "error-free,"
and as a perfect role model for others serve?
Will the use of excuses improve my performances,
or will they cripple and render me ineffective?
One grows stronger by correcting mistakes,
but this cannot be done unless of the errors one is aware.
So why do we deny the truth by attributing blame to others,
when the failure with us lies?

Do not we realize that this only compounds the problems,
causing additional scapegoats for us to look?
In assuming leadership in any cause,
the consequences we must foresee,
and regardless of the outcome,
the responsibility be willingly to bear.
Assuming responsibility is a special skill,
which very few ever possess.
Yet, being responsible is a must,
if successful, one expects to be.

An Instrument of Social Justice

An instrument of social justice I must be
and help remove hatred from the land.
Because oppression we must bring to an end,
obligated I am to take a strong stand.
No one deserves to become enriched
at the expense of those whom we oppress.
Against such evils we must constantly fight--
this message never can we over stress.
Let us rid our society of social injustice,
which inflicts harm in so many ways.
It damages the personality of its victims,
and from standards of decency always strays.
Lack of justice tears the nation asunder,
pitting one group against the other.
Because it deprives us of our greatest potential,
social injustice we must quickly smother.
Committed I am to a just society,
and in a loud voice, for it I will speak.
Inequality in society we can rapidly destroy,
if no longer we tolerate oppression of the weak.
Dedicated I am to social justice;
therefore, racial intolerance I will help to end.

All types of hatred we must terminate,
and human rights to all extend.
In the struggle against injustice, I will be a warrior,
and the rights of the oppressed boldly defend.
I will help the weak to obtain its dignity,
so that in our society we all can blend.

Another Time and Place

For too many of us,
there is no time like now,
and there is no place which compares with here.
What is important in our lives in the here and now.
This parochial attitude, notwithstanding,
we were not always here,
and the time has not always been now.
Although each of us is important in a particular way,
life goes on around us,
and various individuals, whether we know them or not,
have serious consequences for our lives.
Likewise, we are affected by events around us--
even those in the remotest areas of the world.
What we see, hear, feel, smell, and taste
are products of many places,
and are the results of efforts of an earlier day.
Because of this, we cannot afford to be complacent.
We must employ knowledge of the past to build the future.
It is also necessary to see ourselves
as parts of a larger world--
a world in which a problem in one place
creates difficulties elsewhere.
Too often we evaluate ourselves without taking into
consideration other times and other places;
therefore, our assessment is lacking in credibility.
Before deciding that the problems which confront us

are the greatest ever and are insurmountable,
we must consider the problems which others face,
and then view ours in the proper perspective.
Yes, there is a need to emphasize the here and now,
but we can be more honest in our appraisal of life,
if we give more thought to other places,
and place greater focus on other times.
Sure, this is the here and now,
but there are other places;
and without a doubt,
there were other times.

Bearers of Our Dreams

Because in our children our future lies,
love we must show them in every way.
With the very best preparation we must endow them,
so that in tomorrow's world they can have their say.
To us, our children are precious;
therefore, for them we desire the best.
Inspiration, in abundance, we must provide
to assure them that they can pass life's test.
If moral values we instill within them,
prepared they will be, temptations to face.
Therefore, when pressure from peers they encounter,
alien principles they will not embrace.
From the evils of the world we cannot insulate them,
because in such an environment they must endure.
But if provided with appropriate guidance,
their triumph over obstacles will be sure.
Our children are God's special gifts to us;
therefore, in no way should they be abused.
Protection we should give them against evil schemers--
so for neglect of this duty be not accused.
Their health and well-being we must safeguard

as from childhood to adulthood they rapidly grow.
Secondary must be our self-seeking pleasures,
while priority to our children we willingly show.
Time and efforts we must invest in them,
with no sacrifice too great to make;
They are our children, whom we love so dearly;
therefore, of the best in life they should partake.
They are the bearers of our long-held dreams,
who, if prepared, will have much to give.
We must assure them of a brighter tomorrow
since it is through them that we will continue to live.

Before This Day is Done

Before this day is done,
A challenge of worth must be won.
A song of gladness our hearts must sing
And a gift of love for the lonely bring.
A moment of joy to end their sorrow
Will help them face a brighter tomorrow.

Before this day is done,
A greater victory must be won.
Food for the hungry we must provide,
For from their plight we cannot hide.
Home for the homeless we must give,
For these dear children too must live.

Before the sun has set today,
Troubled souls must find their way.
Our strong arms can help, their burdens bear,
And our words of comfort can ease their fear.
The victory, we know, can easily be won,
Long before this day is done.

Before this day is done my friend,
A message of love to someone send.
Lend help to those who have fallen behind
And to the hopeless be patient and kind.
Needless suffering we must deplore,
And open for others the golden door.

Beginning of a New Century

A new century has now arrived,
bringing with it both technological advancements
and innovative ideas.
To this new technology we will have to adjust.
We must come to terms with the many complications
which will accompany it.
Because adjustment in many ways will be difficult,
many chose to glide into the new century,
by accepting most of its advancements
while steering clear of its many uncertainties.
By use of this approach,
we failed to accept responsibility for many problems,
as if they did not originate during our generation.
The world which we pass to others will be far from perfect.
Our children, whom we love so dearly, will enjoy technology
which is unbelievable, but they also will encounter
difficulties which we never anticipated.
Many of which will result from our failure to resolve
earlier problems when they confronted us.
It is convenient for us to devise temporary solutions
to get us safely through a particular crisis,
but the roots of the problem remain.
Now that we have entered the 21st Century
we are challenged to demonstrate true love for our children
by addressing problems which we will force upon them;
while simultaneously, preparing them for their tomorrow.

Changes, we must make in our educational system,
to provide training for effective use of new technology.
Also problems of unemployment we will have to address,
since hunger and homelessness are on the rise.
The perennial environmental crisis also will remain;
therefore, greater emphasis we must give to conservation.
And as our nation becomes more diverse in population,
so must it become in regard to the fruits of opportunity.
Upon other major crises, we must also focus,
and efforts should be made with them to cope.
Welcome has been the 21st Century,
and with it we have to deal.
Let it be a time of innovation.
Let it be a time of hope.

Bridging the Gap

Urgent is the need to bridge the gaps,
which in so many ways have divided us.
They have deprived us of much needed energy,
causing our survival as a nation to be at stake.
Creative strategies we must employ
in order to prevent additional divides.
Greater emphasis we must place on equal opportunities,
with our political system assuming the lead.
Then, gaps we can close which exist among classes,
and fewer will be persons on the two extremes.
Friction between races needs not be so intense,
if interracial ties we more fully embrace.
When racial segregation we cast aside,
a more pluralistic nation we can bring into play.
Numerous are the religions which exist in our nation,
and in peace they all should be able to live.
Intolerance among them they should discard,
and in harmony exist for the good of humankind.

Rural and urban dwellers complement one another,
    and the survival of each on the other depends.
Their working together can be facilitated,
    if mutual respect each shows for the other.
Labor and management should exist as friends
    since common problems together they face.
If they combine efforts to make their products competitive
    in a global economy, their earnings can increase.
The old and young should learn to live together
    since a common home they often must share.
If each, the life style of the other respects,
    their quality of life they can jointly enhance.
Since antagonistic groups in a single nation live,
    tolerance they need in order to survive.
Diverse people can in peace reside
    when gaps among them exist no more.

Who is willing to be a bridge builder?
And find joy in the breaking down of barriers
Significant roles each of us can play
    in bridging the gaps that now divide us.

Champion of a Cause

I have not come to oppose your views,
    nor have I come to condemn you,
    or to call you names.
I have come to state my cause.
I have come to propose a course of action,
    one that I perceive to be positive in nature.
So strong and convincing is my argument,
    that I need not focus upon the weaknesses of yours.
Although you are opposing my views,
    you are not my enemy.
I can never take comfort in your defeat and humiliation.

I have not come to destroy you,
nor the positions which you hold so dearly.
I have come only to champion my cause,
and because I consider it to be a worthy one,
I feel that it can rest on its own merit.
Therefore, if by my argument your ideas are defeated,
it will not be because of my criticisms of your views,
but because of the strength of what I am proposing.
It is not enough for me to destroy your ideas.
It is more important that whatever survives--
survives because it is the best which can be offered.
The winning proposal should provide a solution
to the problem which is being considered.
Therefore, it is not the destruction of the bad which I seek.
It is the triumph of that which is good.
So I come not to oppose or condemn your views.
I come, primarily, to champion my cause--
a cause which I believe to be just.

Changing Society

If the entire society is in need of change,
too heavy is the burden for you to bear.
While the global mission you cannot undertake,
numerous are the needs that are very near.
Major problems are composed of many that are small,
which are less complicated when each stands alone.
If solutions you can find for those that are minor,
then, you can challenge the major ones to be-gone.
More effective you will be in achieving your goal,
if you are willing to narrow your scope.
Have lofty dreams of changes you can make,
but one by one with your problems cope.
Time for you will be a factor,
since defiance you will find to anticipated change.

Deliberate you must be in revisions that are drastic
since many will regard them as being strange.
Dream often of improving the world,
but to a limited cause your efforts devote.
If you are successful in your limited undertaking,
solutions which you offer, others will note.
Therefore, in your efforts to change society,
a successful start you would have made.
Because the patterns you set, others will follow,
major problems of society will begin to fade.

Choosing Our Causes

Numerous are the causes that are worthy,
but with only a few can we fully identify.
For identification calls for a true commitment,
especially when others on us rely.
Modest support we can offer to many efforts,
but serious involvements we must limit to a few.
Committed we must be to the completion of a mission,
rather than championing everything that is new.
Causes we fight for should be chosen with care,
since for them we may have to suffer great pain.
Because with limited resources we are endowed,
restricted should be the goals we struggle to obtain.
For all good causes our assistance is solicited,
but to many requests we must reluctantly decline.
To spread our energy over too many endeavors
will our primary causes seriously undermine.
We must select our causes because of our interests,
and not because they are projects of a friend.
Dedication we must show for our chosen mission,
by pursuing it with full vigor until the end.

Commitment to Service

Are we committed to performing services
to enhance the society in which we live,
or are we among those who expect to be paid
for services to others which we render?
To humanity, do we not owe a debt
for the various benefits which we've received?
Will we respond with a helping hand,
or for more aid for self, will we appeal?
There are so many ways in which we can serve.
So much we have from which we can share.
Our talents in abundance we can employ.
From our rich harvest to others we can give.
On society, we should try not be a burden;
instead, the loads of others we must relieve.
Any assistance we give to help another,
will aid the society in which we live.
Of humanity, we are vital parts;
therefore, for this blessing, thanks we should give.
Because so much of its riches we daily partake,
obligations to its enhancement we should fulfill.
If we do our best to raise its standards,
then, a better life each can enjoy.
So a commitment to service let us make,
for in helping humanity, it is to ourselves that we give.

Constitutional Rights of Blacks

Three-fifth of a man a slave was defined.
This in the Constitution was "underlined."
The Dred Scott decision was another setback.
It denied citizenship to many who were black.
Through the Thirteenth Amendment slaves were freed
from plantation owners who were full of greed.

Citizenship was granted through Amendment Fourteen,
but many blacks questioned what did it mean.
The Fifteenth Amendment expanded the right to vote.
Political rights for blacks is sought to promote.
In later years, the rights of blacks were lost
and had to be recovered at a very high cost.
Plessy v. Ferguson did blacks much harm,
causing civil rights advocates great alarm.
To the Supreme Court many new cases were taken,
causing Jim Crow laws to be weaken and shaken.
Brown v. Board of Education was a historic case
that for the struggle for equality formed a new base.
"Separate but equal" the Court did reject.
It ordered the government all rights to protect.
Then, emerged the Civil Rights Revolution
to give true meaning to the Constitution.
Our March on Washington was a great success
that received the attention of the world-wide press.
Congress then, passed the Civil Rights Act,
that upon segregation had a major impact.
Even though bold action by our government was taken,
our segregated society was barely shaken.
So a great task for us will for a while remain,
until a society of fairness, at last, we obtain.
If this we do as the new century begins,
we can cast away many historic sins.

Diminishing the Violence

Why is there so much violence in society today?
Are we convinced that it has a proper place?
Do we employ violence for our protection,
or because of it, is more protection needed?
Violence spawns violence and this is repeated;
therefore, in our society a vicious cycle is formed.

Violence exists for a variety of reasons,
and in existence it has been from the very beginning.
It is pervasive, being found throughout the world--
in an isolated home and in the global community.
Although to end violence will require a miracle,
for its abatement an effort we must begin.
It is employed by some because of greed,
who after being the victors are victims again.
For the losers seek to redress the wrong,
by using violence their losses to regain.
The loss may be property or it may be pride,
which they seek to recapture at any price.
Because the system provides no adequate redress,
helplessly and hopelessly to violence many turn.
Often against society the revenge is directed;
rather than against those who committed the wrong.
What is gained by the pursuing of violence?
Cannot society a better method find?
Why not a system that will guarantee justice
for those whom by others have been deprived?
When justice is assured to the victims of crime,
violence for revenge can be cast aside;
Therefore, a trend can be set into motion,
causing all acts of violence to begin to decline.
If a society is built where justice is ensured,
perhaps, in a world of less violence we then can live.

Directions

I am not searching for directions,
for I know which road I plan to travel.
Carefully developed are my goals in life,
and I am determined my course to pursue.
Encouragement from you I surely can use
since it will inspire me my goals to reach.

But directions I do not seek,
    for I know which way I plan to travel.

I know what I want to achieve in life,
    and many years for it I have planned.
I am aware of the many obstacles,
    and to confront them I am prepared.
Advice you can give me on strategies to use
    in the achievement of my lofty aims.
Because you have traveled this road before,
    of the impediments in life you are aware.

Know in life your destination,
    and plan ahead your map for travel.
Become aware of the many road blocks,
    but never let them destroy your plans.
Many discouraging words you'll hear
    as others try to chart your course.
But from your goal be not detoured--
    know the direction in which to go.

Diversity in a Pluralistic Society

In the diverse nation in which we live,
    there are people of every race, creed and gender.
Various economic levels are represented,
    and people of all ages can be found.
From throughout the world we have come
    to make this land a "nation of nations".
Our various cultures we have together blended
    to give rare riches to this great country.
The pluralistic society in which we live
    poses no major problem for national unity,
    since on basic principles we agree.
To the contrary, our diversity strengthens us.

It brings to this nation a variety of experiences.
It is useless to insist on a homogeneous culture,
even though numerous advantages it appears to have.
Given, however, our national composition,
such an experiment would in failure end.
A nation of diversity we must continue to build,
where there exists no dominant culture,
and in locked steps we are not required to march.
Instead, each sub-culture, in a manner that is unique,
contributes to the quilting of the American way.
In this process, we cannot afford to be intolerable,
rather, we must demonstrate an understanding and
appreciation of cultures of all of our people.
Their extrinsic values we must recognize.
Superiority of culture, let no group lay claim,
for subjective is the instrument
by which such judgment is made.
Satisfaction should be derived from groups,
which conclude that their cultural traits
are functional and meet their respective needs.
Their ways of life are neither better nor worse
than those of others;
therefore, a single culture needs not be perceived
as the one which we all should embrace;
nor should one's culture be rejected as being contrary
to the "American way."
Suffice it to say, ethnic cleansing has no place in our society.
Diversity, for us, is not an option,
but a necessity in our pluralistic nation.

Education

Education can open doors,
allowing individuals to be free.
It can liberate them from enslavement,

and enable them a better world to see.
New opportunities it creates,
permitting us to achieve long-sought dreams.
With the many skills it provides us,
we can be leaders of challenging teams.
Education gives us confidence
that in our fields we can succeed.
It equips us with an expertise,
that gives us a voice that others will heed.
Education prepares us for earning a living.
Skills for us it can provide.
It lays a foundation on which to build.
It will enable us to maintain the stride.
Education can be an equalizer.
A fairer society it can help us to make.
Barriers to opportunities it can remove;
therefore, of the fruits of society we all can partake.
Education, we should always pursue,
since it is never too late to learn.
Because of its potential value,
always for it we should yearn.

End of a Century

For the benefits of the 20th Century, we are thankful.
since so many improvements in our lives it has made.
We witnessed breakthroughs which we did not anticipate,
but innumerable problems we also faced.
The world became a global community,
with transportation and communications opening doors.
Many things they rendered antiquated,
and accompanying the changes were problems galore.
The conquest of the air we considered amazing,
with a variety of functions being served by planes.
They gave new meaning to the pursuing of warfare,

and international travel became an overnight affair.
The space age moved us another step forward,
with our neighborhood expanding beyond the earth.
Astronauts landed on the moon's surface,
and neighboring planets came within our reach.
Computers reduced our need to travel,
since from our homes, with the world we could deal.
Satellites brought us many innovations;
thus, facilitating contact with people afar.
While advanced technology brought us closer together,
it also was a cause for our drifting apart.
We became neighbors with peoples in distant lands,
who seemed as if they lived next door.
But it gave us less need for local interactions;
thus, people in the community we didn't get to know.
Television and computers occupied our time;
therefore, in our home we were contented to stay.
So advanced technology was for us a blessing,
but in many ways a curse, as well.
Nevertheless, the century was productive,
and with its problems we learned to live.
So as we enter the 21st Century,
over the past we pause to reflect.
Thankful, we are for our many experiences,
which provide a prelude of what is yet to come.

Entering the 21st Century

Now that we have entered the 21st Century,
pursue we will our newly drawn plan.
There are difficult problems which we must solve,
and by employing our skills we surely can.
A myriad of new problems we now will confront,
but first we must resolve those that are old.
If we are to prevent them from further expansion,

solutions we apply must be bold.
There is so much in life which we anticipate,
now that the new century has arrived.
However, from the old one we can build
from that of value which survived.
So a tribute we pay to the passing century,
with the good in life which to us it brought.
With progress, however, came many new problems;
therefore, valuable lessons to us it taught.
So thankful we are for the Twenty-First Century,
and for our many dreams which we expect to fulfill.
Because we continue to strive for a brighter tomorrow,
Forward! We must move, We cannot stand Still.

Environmental Concerns

Our environment is a place of beauty,
which God created to be enjoyed by all.
Of this beauty we can daily partake
without reducing it to needless spoil.
Rich is the earth in natural resources,
which are placed under our domain.
For the good of humanity let us use them,
but from unnecessary abuse, we must refrain.
Not to us alone do these riches belong,
but to generations that are yet to come.
Upon natural resources they will strongly depend;
therefore, for their survival, concern we must show.
Not for human alone was the world created,
but for everything which on earth do dwell.
For animals God provided space;
therefore, in their domain let us not tread.
Because our environment to all belong,
our selfish motives we should restrain.
Concern we must have for more than our pleasure,

if a world of beauty we are to maintain.

Everyone's a Teacher

From the teacher students partake their knowledge.
They learn from the instruction which to them that is given,
and in the process they also learn by observation.
While what is taught is a meaningful lesson,
so are the experiences which the students encounter.
We learn from those who have been taught to teach,
and we learn from those whom we consider untrained.
In essence, everyone is a teacher,
and lessons are taught by all whom we meet.
An arrogant minister preaches a lesson of arrogance,
and a loafer symbolizes the meaning of laziness.
A generous neighbor teaches a lesson of kindness,
and a wise old man gives us a display of wisdom.
All around us lessons are taught,
and from all around us lessons are learned.
We learn to be responsible fathers,
but we learn also to shirk our duties.
We learn to be kind and ever forgiving,
and we learn to be greedy and full of hate.
We learn to be honest and just in our dealings,
and we learn to be sinister and very notorious.
We acquire knowledge on mildness and humility,
and we learn to be loud and filled with conceit.
To uplift humanity we have been taught,
but to degrade other humans we have learned, as well.
Dual messages to us our teachers send,
but we decide for ourselves our response.
Everyone is a student who is eager to learn,
and everyone is a teacher with a lesson to teach.
So we must be aware of the instructions we give,
and also mindful of the lives we live.

Teachers often teach from a designed plan,
    but students learn from wherever they can.
Everyone is a teacher who always teaches.
Everyone is a teacher who has no bounds.

Exclude None

Others into the system must be brought
    if our nation is to achieve its best.
United must be our national efforts
    if a greater nation we are to become.
All persons must be given the chance,
    their opinions to freely express.
Our nation is made stronger
    when attention is given to the smallest protest.
We cannot afford to ostracize
    those whose races are different from ours.
Exclusion should never our policy be
    in a democracy where we all are free.
Minority concerns, the system must address
    and a response give to their pressing needs.
Problems at times, must be resolved
    even before the demands are perceived.
Into the government we must integrate
    voices of every race, gender and creed.
The national fiber we can strengthen
    if, into one beautiful quilt we all are woven.
So power is not to be shared by a few,
    when the decisions affect us all.
We must encourage others to have their say
    and induce them to contribute to the cause.
If we tap our full resources,
    we can build a nation strong and free.
Therefore, let us keep our democracy alive,
    by employing a system which excludes none.

Falling Apart

All that is around us cannot fall apart.
There must be something in which to believe.
Our major institutions cannot all deceive us.
Inspiration from somewhere we must receive.
In our government, can we place our trust?
Will it the best interest of the nation serve,
 or will the politicians seek only self-advancement;
 therefore, from ethical behavior always swerve?
Long long ago we discredited big business,
 realizing that money only it sought to gain.
Loudly, it proclaims its concern for the public,
 while greater profits it continues to obtain.
Various professions disregard their ethics,
 and with new rules play their games.
Some of the practices which they observe
 only serve to disgrace their names.
Colleges and universities we often criticize,
 because proper leadership they do not provide.
When over-emphasis of sports ends in scandal
 from their lack of integrity, they try to hide.
Religious institutions also have deceived us,
 as for monetary gains they continue to reach.
Minimal service they perform for the needy,
 but this is not the sermon which to us they preach.
What has happened to our once stable families?
Do they still have roles in which to play?
Do various members perform as a team,
 or has each decided that that doesn't pay?
Institutions appear to be falling apart,
 with their roles being left for others to fill.
To pessimism, however, we cannot surrender,
 for with proper reform we can cure this ill.
Although it seems to us that we are doomed,
 there remains for us a glimmer of hope.

During the 21st Century, faith we must have
that with the matter of integrity we can better cope.

Filling the Vacuum

Someone must fill the vacuums in life,
which if left unfilled will encourage strife.
Someone must be willing to take the lead,
if not the battle we will have to concede.
Someone must be ready to take a stand,
by assuming responsibilities and taking command.
Those who do, deserve our applause
for sacrifices they make for a noble cause.
The voids in life we must fill--
new life into programs we must instill.
Revitalized goals we must pursue,
with innovative efforts that are long overdue.
New ideas are needed to replace the old,
and the action we take must be swift and bold.
Voids in life cannot any longer remain,
since in our lives they cause added strain.
Fillers of vacuums usually are abused,
and by others they are often accused
of having concealed goals for which they aim,
and seeking to exploit for self-acclaim.
Have little concern for what others say--
they contribute so little, but seek to have their way.
Credit you deserve for the action you took,
when the dying cause most others forsook.

Flow of Creative Ideas

There must be a flow of creative ideas,
    if we are to continue to thrive.
Among us there must be visionaries,
    who can challenge us to achieve our best.
Survival to us should not mean merely existing,
    for to current demands we must rise.
If only to the past we continue to respond,
    can our existence be justified?
Therefore, let us search for creative ideas--
    for innovations, which are not yet out-of-date;
    for designs that will challenge our imaginations
    and push us to be more than we ever dreamed.
An excellence can be achieved that will astound us,
    and our model of success can be a guide.
Success in our endeavors will be guaranteed,
    and justification we'll have for why we survive.
From where will come these creative ideas?
Upon our present pool of resources can we rely?
Sure, there are those among us who dare to dream,
    but too narrow usually are their perspectives.
Because we have restricted ourselves to the here and now,
    from outside our walls innovations must come.
To the young and inspired we must turn--
    to those whose dreams remain unfulfilled.
To many of us, they will appear to be rebels,
    since the status quo they will surely challenge.
Rebels they are not; however,
    but our antiquated system they will reject.
A part of our team they seek to be,
    and by cooperative efforts achieve success.
Welcome should be their flow of new ideas,
    which by us can be adequately tested.
Rejection of creative minds we cannot afford,
    if our continued existence we truly seek.

Either we accept young thinkers into our fold,
    or be members of their creative teams.

Flowers Not Weeds

Too many flowers have turned into weeds,
    although they germinated from very good seeds.
If they had been provided the proper care,
    we would have had blooms that are very rare.
Instead, they were recklessly allowed to grow
    in competition with weeds which we did not sow.
Now these flowers, their beauty have lost,
    but could have been saved at a reasonable cost.

Let no flower around us turn into a weed,
    because of encouragement which we did not feed.
Let not the flowers the weeds destroy,
    because of adequate care we did not employ.
Beautiful flowers, great efforts deserve.
We must treat them well and their beauty preserve.
Let not their beauty fade away,
    since we need it here to "make our day."

Children of beauty we should try to save,
    for they had potentials when to us God gave.
Into thorns and thistles they must not stray;
    thus, weeds of temptation must be kept away.
No one we should allow our children to steal,
    for the beauty they possess truly is real.
If this beauty in children we preserve,
    the good of humanity they later will serve.

Freedom to Discuss

On virtually every issue there are schools of thought,
    and before acceptance there are battles to be fought.
Many have ideas they endeavor to project
    in order on proposals to have an effect.
So be not adamant in the views you hold,
    others have ideas in which to unfold.
Let each idea on its merit be judged.
Evaluate each carefully, we should be urged.

Views of others we must not repress,
    nor should one dominate and talk in excess.
Discussions should be held in an environment that's free.
Intolerance of others should never be.
Dissident views we should fully explore,
    even though their authors we do not adore.
Value in their proposals, occasionally, can be found.
The ideas they offer can sometimes be sound.

So look not at the person, but examine the fact,
    and use good judgment before you react.
The ideas you offer are among the best,
    when compared with others they pass the test.
Good they are, but perfect they are not,
    so time for discussion to others allot.
Be not disturbed if some disagree,
    for that is their right in discussions that are free.

We came tonight not to be told,
    but on new ideas to be sold.
So state your views and state them with pride.
    and after we have heard them we will decide.
Feel not that we are standing on the brink,
    merely because we are beginning to think.

For decisions should be made in a democratic way,
where all have the right to have their say.

From the Sea Shore

From the sea shore with sadness, I watched
as nations in Europe engaged in war.
While the United States pondered its eventual entry,
in the name of freedom millions died.

From the shores of Africa with sadness, I watched
the route to America which my ancestors took.
In overcrowded ships as slaves they traveled,
and many died wanting to be free.

From the American shore with gladness, I watched
as a new Africa emerged upon the scene.
Making their exit were the colonial powers,
as millions gained their right to be free.

From the shore I watched with mixed emotions
the ocean which was so clear and blue.
It was the sea which the pilgrims traveled
as they came to this country in order to be free.

Also, it was the ocean which trade ships crossed
to introduce slavery on the American scene.
Happiness it brought to the plantation owners,
but disaster for those who were not free.

This sea at times, has been one of calmness,
and at other times it has been a scene of storms.
Millions have crossed it in anticipation--
in hope of making this country their home.

Others have crossed it with great anxiety,
knowing not what would be their fate.
The journey of the pilgrims was quite successful,
but the tragedy of the slaves was a national disgrace.

From the sea shore I watch, once again,
and for a better world I continue to dream--
Of peace and happiness for those beyond,
and contentment for us who live within.

Gatekeepers

In virtually every phase of life,
we find those who are within the gates,
and those who remain outside the walls.
To be inside is the goal of many of the outsiders.
They seek to enter in order to enjoy
what they perceive to be the good life.
The desire to enter, however, is quite different
from being allowed to enter.
Who is to enter is a decision
to be made by those within the gates,
and not by those who seek entrance.
Gatekeepers have been designated to grant entry
to those whom they determine to be worthy,
and to reject those whom they perceive as lacking
in credentials.
Yes, it is the gatekeepers who decide.
They make decisions concerning the receivers of degrees,
and they guard the entry into professions.
They decide the organizations' membership,
and they determine by whom the system will be run.
The gatekeepers are those who possess power,
and they will make decisions concerning every phase of life.

They determine our successes,
and they can bring about our downfall.
Because they are the gatekeepers you can enter into their choice domain only by their permission.
They are the haves who possess what you want.
They are the incumbents, whom you seek to replace.
They are the bestowals of the credentials which you need.
They are those who stand at the gate.
They are those to whom you must cater if you are to enter.
They are loved and they are despised.
They have friends whom they have helped,
and they have enemies whose lives they have destroyed.
They are "regular people," they say,
but your future is in their hands.
They are the gatekeepers--
those at the gate through which you must enter.
They are the gatekeepers.

Global is Our Community

Global is our community.
In one small village we now seem to live.
Obstacles which for centuries have kept us apart;
by modern technology have been removed.
No longer is transportation a divisive factor.
No place in the world seems more than a day away.
And communication with once far-away neighbors
now with household microwaves favorably compares.
Indeed, these advancements have made our world smaller,
but not without a cost did this closeness come.
Are we bearers only of the fruits of progress,
or are there also consequences which we must face?
Since global is our community,
with universal matters we must be concerned.
For interrelated are our various activities,

with each on the other having a serious impact.
A disruption of peace in a far away place,
becomes a problem which we too must address.
The hunger and homelessness which it produces,
within our nation will also cause distress.
By such remote events, many lives are touched,
and even though we know so little about those
who are directly involved,
in a very personal way we, too, are victims.
In our small world we are not mere observers;
but participants in the on-going struggle for power.
Therefore, with seriousness we ask:
How close are we to global disaster,
because of international problems left unresolved?
Harmonious living in our global community,
will on each of us depend.

Heed the Cry of the Needy

Throughout the world there are people in need.
and of their existence we are aware.
Everyday they cry out to us for help,
but their pleas we refuse to heed.
Outside of our view we try to hide them.
With invisible walls they are concealed.
Their plight we ignore as long as we can--
considering their problems to be unreal.

In our communities there are pleas for help,
which go unheeded virtually everyday.
We cannot pretend that we do not hear them,
for our lives are disrupted by their cries of distress.
Why must the needy be turned aside,
when we have so much from which to give?

Why can't we lend our helping hands
    to help the oppressed another day to live?

Let us not build walls around them,
    in order our consciences to keep clean.
We must help alleviate their suffering,
    for this tragedy we cannot conceal.
Why deprive those who are suffering,
    when their burdens we can relieve?
We can bring hope to those who languish,
    by a gesture of humanity which we extend.

Honesty as Our Trademark

Let honesty be our trademark,
    that will help us our character define.
Let it ignite a special spark
    that will make it easier to tow the line.
It will help us in peace to live
    with all whom we happen to meet.
It will lessen the need for others to forgive;
    therefore, making for all a life that is sweet.

Let honesty be the policy we use
    in business activities which we undertake.
Let us not another abuse
    by dishonest statements which we make.
Cheating never should be our aim,
    for it profits us not in the end.
Let us earn that for which we claim.
On honesty only should we depend.

Dishonesty can bring us shame;
    therefore, from it there is much to learn.

When we, too, are victims of the game,
for integrity then, our hearts will yearn.
So honesty, let us always employ,
and through it our honor retain,
Rather than ourselves destroy,
and on our record leave a stain.

In Anticipation

Millions wait in anticipation
to witness the beginning of a brighter day.
For years they have prayed for a better tomorrow,
but it always seems to be delayed.
Nothing appears to be going their way
as from day to day they struggle to live.
Therefore, in anticipation they sit and wait
for the tomorrow of which they have dreamed.
Old baggage they would like to cast aside,
and with a clean slate begin anew.
If only yesterday they can forget,
fresh hope they can find on which to build.
Yes, millions wait in anticipation--
for the new century to arrive.
Confidence they have that solutions we'll find
to critical problems which confuse their minds.
If to the search we remain committed,
the termination of racial hatred we can begin.
We can minimize the impact of population explosion,
and curtail poverty and its many effects.
Violence in society we can seriously diminish
and environmental abuse we can make scarce to find.
World peace, which remains our most cherished dream,
can in this new century become alive.
Hope, we have for medical breakthroughs
that will enable us, cures to find.

Advanced technology will enable us to cope
with the myriad of problems we didn't have before.
So thanks be to God for the things of the past.
which prepared us for what lies ahead.
His guidance we'll need as this new century we face;
thus, with great anticipation we wait--
Wait, for the century of hope.

In Charge of My Destiny

In charge of my destiny I have chosen to be,
even if against the tide I will have to swim.
All obstacles I am prepared to face,
whether new or from years of the past.
Throughout history, struggles have been waged,
and there have been obstacles which had to be overcome.
Some chose to go over, under, and around them,
while others undertook the more serious challenge
of removing them.
Those who chose to dislodge them were aware that
in destroying these enemies of success,
they were making it easier for those who are to follow.
Understanding the impediments to success makes it easier
for one to confront them effectively;
and by doing so, obtain those things which others
regard as unobtainable.
If there are goals in life which I seriously seek,
then I must be willing to exert the energy needed
to achieve them.
Fully investing myself in the cause must be my top priority.
So intense must be my efforts that obstacles cannot deter me.
If the goal I seek is of major consequence,
then, I must be willing to sacrifice in proportion.
I know the meaning of hard work and I must apply it;
for to be a party to my defeat, I cannot afford.

Influenced by my environment I will always be,
    but others will never be allowed my course to determine.
With faith in God, my dreams are pursued,
    and their accomplishment, by his grace, I will achieve.
Because with wisdom and strength He will endow me,
    in charge of my destiny will be left to me.

In Search of Peace

In a peaceful world I want to live,
    where strife is seldom found.
Where no nation needs to be aggressive
    for only within its boundary each seeks to survive.
Concerned will be each with domestic improvements,
    as their standards of living each will try to raise.
Social problems will become their major priority.
    as internal peace each will strive to maintain.
In a peaceful nation I want to live
    where social justice exists for all.
Where crime, no longer, is a major threat,
    and the police officer is merely a friend.
In peace within my community, I want to live--
    where friction exists as a thing of the past.
A place where neighbors will together work
    to enhance their communities in every way.
At peace with myself I want to be,
    with very few wars to fight within.
Content I want to be with decisions I make;
    so that free from distress and in peace I can live.

In Search of Racial Understanding

How do we achieve better racial understanding?
At what point should our efforts begin?
Although the search may be long-lasting,
    initially, we should search deep within.
Do we harbor hatred for those around us--
    those who may be of another race?
Have we arrived at unsubstantiated conclusions,
    and because of this, racial hatred embrace?
By understanding ourselves we can understand each other;
    therefore, better conclusions we can draw.
We'll realize that those around us are less than perfect,
    but we, too, are not without a flaw.
Those of other races have peculiarities,
    which we do not always understand.
But do not be quick to denounce their cultures
    since in control of them we have no command.
We must be broad-minded in judging others,
    rather than parochial in the opinions we hold.
Much about other cultures we need to learn--
    stories of their successes are often not told.
Interaction with other races is a must
    in this pluralistic society in which we share.
When more about others we understand,
    for their problems we'll show greater care.

Innovation

We are in search of a person with new ideas--
    a person who possesses a creative mind;
    one who is prepared for innovations;
    society is in need of such a find.
How long will we endure the status quo?

Unworkable traditions we must cast aside.
If no useful purpose they continue to serve,
    why by them do we still abide?
New situations require new solutions
    which unfortunately have not been found;
    therefore, our search for innovators--
    who to the past will not be bound.
Old concepts need to be re-examined,
    and that of value we can still embrace;
    but much innovation by society is needed,
    if current evils we are to erase.
So, serious is our search for innovators--
    persons who can help us bring about change;
    persons who can help us solutions to find,
    and much of society help to rearrange.
Step forward if you are innovative.
We are in need of your creative mind.
To society, you will be a blessing.
Thank you for being one of a kind.

Judging of Others

In the world in which we live, there are peoples
    of many races, ethnic groups and religious backgrounds.
Each in a special way has something to give,
    and each has characteristics which leave much to be desired.
Too often, however, we are apt to generalize,
    but generalizing we should not do, since persons should be considered independently of the groups in which they belong.
We should judge people on their merit,
    and if this is done,
    we will find acceptable friends in all groups.
Likewise, we will meet persons with detestable traits in each.

In our judging of others we must try to consider their orientations, and not necessarily ours.
We must remember that because people come from different backgrounds,
their responses should not be expected to be the same as ours.
We must make allowances for their idiosyncrasies in the same way in which others have overlooked our faults.
They, too, seek forgiveness for their mistakes
just as we should seek forgiveness for those we make
We should not despise persons because of their race,
religion, ethnic group, or other persuasions.
Instead, we should love them because of their attributes,
which should outweigh their particular group identification.
If we judge others by the same standards by which we are judged,
we will find that interacting with others in a multi-cultural world
can be a rewarding experience.

Lending a Helping Hand

On my broad shoulder I want to share
the burdens of the tired, the weak and oppressed.
Those whose battles forever seem hopeless.
Those who have lost again and again.
No longer do they entertain a grain of optimism
that on solid ground they will ever stand.
From day to day they eke out a living,
knowing not what tomorrow will bring.
To my brothers and sisters I have a hand to lend,
when in trouble they are deeply entrenched.
Perhaps, bridges for them I can help to build
that to the other side will enable them to cross.
There, prosperity may greet them,

and a new life permit them to start.
Let me contribute to their enhancement,
by the helping hand which I extend.
Because by God, I have been so richly blessed;
with the unfortunate I can easily share.
Their burdens I truly know,
for down this road I have walked myself.
There were times when I was full of doubt,
with obstacles confronting me on every side,
but across troubled waters I was assisted,
so now to the helpless a hand I'll lend.

Making an Impact

Upon society are you making an impact,
through various endeavors which you're pursuing?
Are you finding joy in your challenging pursuits,
or are they ordeals that you are merely enduring?
Think of your work as laying a foundation
for those who later must travel this road.
In some way are you making a contribution
to help relieve tomorrow's heavy load?
Are you seeking to develop solutions
that will the next generation serve;
that will help resolve complicated problems
and menaces of society begin to unnerve?
Are you seeking to be creative,
and will leave behind you works of art?
Will you leave some lasting reminders
that for humanity you did your part?
Will your life be an inspiration
that will for others a light provide?
Will the story which you have written
be for the doubtful a useful guide?

Upon life make an impact,
that will account for years, here, you've spent.
History, then, will record that you lived
and affected humanity to a substantial extent.

Making Democracy a Reality

In the name of democracy let us build a nation strong.
Let us open its doors to all who dwell therein.
Let us assure each the right of participation--
the right to share in the making of a great nation
and the right to partake of the many riches it produces.
So important is participation in the affairs of a democracy
that every step must be taken to involve each in the process.
Indeed, such participation is essential to its success.
Because of the need for active participation on the part of all,
it is not feasible merely to open the doors
and await volunteers;
instead, we must take the initiative and usher into government
those who can make a difference--
those who can bring to us innovative ideas
and can help solve the critical problems which confront us.
Likewise, we must make use of those, who for so long
have been regarded as having nothing to give.
A closer look will reveal that they, too, play a vital role
in the perpetuation of democracy.
To fail to open doors is to guarantee the diminishing of the
quality of the nation and our cherished form of government.
Rare talent, which we have not recognized, will be denied us,
causing less prepared persons to assume critical positions
in our society.
This is not the course that true democrats must follow.
To all who live here there must be an open door--
an open door for service and an open door to enjoy
the fruits of the nation.

Democracy comes alive not only when the majority has its way,
but also when the rights of minorities are well protected.
It should never be the intent of the majority to disregard
the interest of the minority,
since the latter can make valuable contributions to the
well-being of the nation.
Indeed, the success of a democracy can be judged by the degree
to which the majority approaches unanimity.
Thus, a majority, in safeguarding its own interest, should seek
to bring as many dissidents into the fold, as possible.
Not only should it encourage the incorporation of other ideas,
it should also be about the task of soliciting them.
In order for our democracy to be sustained,
we must constantly infuse it with new ideas
and new personnel.
Likewise, democracy must prove itself capable of coping
with the numerous new problems which confront it.
Democracy does not just survive on its own merit,
but, because its adherents are devoted to its survival.
It will achieve its fulfillment only when we rid it of its many
defects.
This we can do by substituting inclusion for exclusion--
a policy which for too long has been the established practice
of the nation.
To continue our present course is to invite disaster,
and the responsibility for this will be attributed to
the unwillingness of the advocates of democracy
to make it a reality.
Democracy must survive and its maximal potentials achieved.

Measures of Adulthood

Let not others your adulthood define,
    by arbitrary standards which they have designed.
Never their expectations feel obligated to meet,
    if lower moral values for you they prescribe.
Sexual exploitation defines not adulthood,
    nor one's ability to create a child.
Involvement in drugs does not a grown-up make,
    even though rewarding seems the financial gains.
Cigarette smoking implies not maturity,
    your manhood or womanhood it does not define.
Your peers may advise you alcohol to consume,
    but grown-up status it will not bring.
The wielding of a gun may give the impression
    that a man or woman you may have become.
As a youth, again, you will long to be,
    when as an adult in prison, you will be confined.
Why the rush to achieve adulthood?
On whom are you seeking an impression to make?
Are you ready to put your youth behind you?
A more mature status are you willing to assume?
When adulthood you eventually achieve,
    of its awareness you will have no doubt.
Crucial decisions you will be called upon to make,
    and responsibility for your actions you will have to take.

Menaces to Society

Against the menaces of society we must stand guard,
    for harmful are their effects on humankind.
As perpetrators of evil, they have established records;
    thus, aware we are of their dastardly styles.
Clandestinely, they usually devise their schemes,
    in order their victims to spring a surprise.

If however, on guard we will be,
    minimize we can their disastrous effects.
Poverty is among the major menaces,
    which undermines society in so many ways.
From unemployment it has often emanated,
    and hunger and homelessness it leaves in its wake.
Racism is also a menace with longevity.
So much anguish to the nation it has brought.
National unity it often disrupts,
    preventing harmonious relations where it is a must.
Vital human resources it denies society,
    preventing talented individuals from contributing their best.
The nation, it keeps on the brink of disaster,
    with threats of riots becoming a reality.
Religious intolerance is another menace,
    with roots in history so deeply imbedded.
The cause of international warfare long it has been,
    and it has threatened to tear many nations asunder.
Violence pervades virtually every society,
    causing us to live in perpetual fear.
It is exhibited in constant warfare,
    where lives of millions continue to be lost.
Prevalent it is in every community,
    where the daily news it dominates
In our homes it is a major problem,
    where the term "family" has meaning no more.
How do we eliminate these four great menaces?
For answers to these problems where do we turn?
Because in society, they are well entrenched;
    against these evils we must take a stand.

Millions on the March

There are millions on the march again,
in search of a better life.
They are victims of needless wars.
They are oppressed minorities,
and they are the hungry seeking food.
A temporary home is what they ask--a place to rest
before continuing their search for a better life.
They are the old, the young and the unborn.
They are the blind, the cripple,
and those who suffer from malnutrition.
During their trek, their babies were born
and their loved ones died.
They are a tragedy in movement,
living in fear wherever they go.
They are pursued by those
from whom they are fleeing,
and they are attacked by those
whose territory they enter.
These refugees know only despair
since their hope was lost long ago.
These homeless people are not strangers to us,
for we see their pictures virtually everyday.
While they are brought close to us
they do not become alive.
We do not feel their pains,
and experience their hopelessness.
They are people whom we visit briefly,
as we change channels on our television sets.
Our changing channels, however,
does not change their conditions,
nor does it erase the fact
that we are aware of their existence.
Realizing that they are among the "least of these,"
we question:

Are they not a part of humanity,
and among those whom we should extend
a helping hand?
This question we ponder again and again,
as millions continue their search
for a permanent home.

Morning

Awake! for now it is morning,
and new challenges we now must face.
Our tasks already have been assigned,
now our duties we must embrace.
Time, we cannot afford to waste,
for we must finish before it's noon.
We will find ourselves behind schedule,
if we do not begin very soon.
If in the coolness of morning we work,
then less we'll sweat from the summer heat.
Energy we will have to complete the task;
thus, there will be no need to think of retreat.
Much we must do during the morning of life,
while our youthfulness we still possess.
By late morning we should be at our best,
and should have experienced our first success.
Few can wait until afternoon,
a significant task to begin.
Too many others would have already started,
who the best things in life most likely will win.
Morning people have time for creativity.
Many experiences they can undertake.
To earlier failures they can make adjustments,
and for challenging opportunities be wide awake.

My Spoken Words

In a soft voice I am going to speak,
    but my words I want to be heard.
A major impact I trust they will make,
    for intended they are for a special effect.
In vociferous language I need not speak,
    in order my point to make.
If my reasoning you are prepared to follow,
    on its merits only should judgment be made.
Few are the words I am prepared to utter,
    and clear in meaning they all will be.
No hidden agenda I am seeking to advance,
    so motives of selfishness attribute not to me.
My words are not intended to impress
    those who extensive vocabularies admire.
In very simple language my argument I'll make;
    therefore, on my words only should I be judged.
No rudeness is intended in the remarks I give.
No insults to others do I wish to imply.
So respect for me I trust that you'll show,
    then, assess only my spoken words.
Judge me not on previous positions,
    or what you anticipated my words would be.
Draw not any preconceived conclusions,
    Wait until you have heard what I have said.

Obstacle in My Own Way Standing

Am I an obstacle in my own way standing
Preventing me from achieving success?
Are significant opportunities am I being denied,
Because of the arrogance which I possess?
Unlimited once seemed what I could achieve
But I pursued my course without tact.

Therefore, friends who could have been helpful,
Chose instead not to act.
My success in life will on me depend.
It is only I who can cause my defeat.
If a change in my attitude I refuse to make
From my treasured goals I will have to retreat.
Why self glorification must I always reflect,
And in a condescending voice to others speak?
Why must I give the impression that I have power,
When in reality I am very weak?
To most of my adversary I am invincible,
But against myself it is difficult to stand
In so many ways I promote self-destruction
For over myself I am not in command.
I am an obstacle in my own way standing;
Therefore, higher goals are difficult to achieve.
Until I make the necessary adjustments
Disaster only I can expect to receive.

Obtaining Respect

Respect is what most of us seek,
whether ascribed or achieved.
In a sense, we earn it at birth,
since in dignity we all were born.
Beyond this level of respect, however,
special recognition is given because of talent.
When admiration is based on ability,
our level of prestige varies
with the quality of our performance.
Thus, around us are many
who were once applauded,
but are now greeted by silence.
Respect also is accorded persons
because of positions held.

To those with superior titles,
subordinates usually give deference.
While in many cases this is superficial,
it can become authentic if to subordinates
proper concern is shown.
In a hierarchical arrangement,
very little emphasis is placed on showing respect
to those at the lower end of the totem pole.
Nevertheless, because they make unique contributions,
they, too, are entitled to respect--
a respect, which no admired superior
will ever fail to show.
Respect based on performances and titles
can very seldom be compared with that
which one earns because of good character.
Such persons are held in high esteem
because of their exemplary behavior.
They are admired because of the attitudes they display
in regards to others.
Since genuine is respect that is based on character
by its recipient it should be highly regarded.
For such admiration, we all should strive.

Opportunity

Opportunity came our way today,
but to it we could not respond.
As a "group" we would have had to work;
but there existed among us no special bond.
Success was achieved by those with unity--
those with a cooperative project to pursue.
Because they knew the art of working together,
the success they received was what was due.

Opportunity knocked, once again, today,
but it left us filled with anger and dismay.
For proper preparation we had not made,
and we could not secure another delay.
Although of the deadline we were well aware,
too long we procrastinated before making a start.
Easy it was to blame someone else,
but really, we had failed to do our part.

Opportunity appeared before us today,
but its offer we refused.
Too involved we were with other activities,
from which we could not readily be excused.
Because too tightly we had made our schedules,
for attractive additions we had no room.
An excellent offer we had to reject--
too involved we were; thus came the gloom.

Our Failures

Why is our society failing in its purpose?
What drastic errors did we make?
Were we blinded by leaders who mislead us?
Of alien philosophies did we partake?
We cannot identify one significant error,
that caused us from our pathway to stray.
There was a series of minor deviations,
that slowly contributed to our decay.
Our simple mistakes when first we made them
were not causes for serious alarm;
but as those errors became compounded,
to our society they inflicted great harm.
Major problems we can see and correct,
before our system they eventually destroy.

But minor mistakes cause slow erosion;
    therefore, corrected solutions we do not employ.
No one person can be held responsible
    for our critical problems which remain unsolved.
Although we would like to place the blame on others,
    in various small ways we too were involved.
Thus, let us not question what's causing our downfall,
    since we contribute to it almost every day.
Slight deviations which we thought wouldn't matter
    are collectively causing us this permanent decay.

Our Heroes and Heroines

Why are these the ones whom we are honoring?
Why are they being given the highest awards?
Do they represent values which we espouse?
Are they the role models for our future stars?
Our heroes and heroines sometimes are formed
    from flimsy material which cannot last.
Because they possess one outstanding quality,
    perfection we attribute in every respect.
But perfect are not our heroes and heroines,
    whose behavior is similar to ours.
Yet disturbed are we when they fall from grace,
    for as flawed role models they now appear.
Why did we ever place them on such high pedestals,
    when we knew, like others, they had their faults?
Was it done only for commercial reasons?
If so, didn't we know that it would not last.
Why is there a need for super stars,
    whom we glorify in every possible way?
Do they rank that high above fellow performers,
    on whose performances they often depend?
Why the famous must we further elevate,
    whose heads, too often, are above the clouds?

Why not aid those who are constantly struggling,
    and help them, their first glory to taste?
In every community there are those who are worthy,
    whose contributions are deserving of praise.
Why not pay them a special tribute,
    and aid the causes for which they stand?
Let us honor a galaxy of stars,
    rather than glorifying only one.
The existence of thousands of living legends
    can better light us the heavenly skies.

Our Homeland

As I visited the land of my ancestors,
    I tried to peer deeply into its past.
I sought to better understand the land where they once lived.
While I was not interested in their status in African society,
    many other questions continued to perplex me.
Did they live cooperatively with their neighbors,
    or were they constantly engaged in confrontation?
Was poverty for them a never-ending cycle,
    or did they live in a land of abundance?
How did they welcome the strangers who invaded their country?
Did they cooperate in these foreign conquests,
    or did they resist stubbornly the invasion of their culture?
Were they willing participants in colonial exploits,
    or did they seek to undermine them whenever possible?
Were Africans enriched by these imperialistic penetrations,
    or was the continent robbed of potential greatness?
Even though it was my desire, I could not revisit the Africa
    of my ancestors.
I could only rely on studies which have analyzed the past.
Unfortunately, too often, they ignored pertinent facts,
    while embellishing others.

Although I am lacking in adequate knowledge of my ancestors,
of my current African kin I am more aware.
From a distance, I observed their emergence on the international
scene, as they formed nation states.
I witnessed, from afar, both their glories and their tragedies.
I applauded their major political and economic accomplishments,
but I bemoaned the numerous civil wars which engulfed too
many new African nations--threatening to tear them
asunder while still in infancy.
My kinship with the continent makes it necessary for me
to identify with its future with the same enthusiasm
as I claim linkage with its past.
The African cause is my cause--
its triumphs are my successes, and its defeats are my
failures.
Their joys bring me exhilaration,
and their sorrows cause me distress.
I cannot prosper while in poverty my kin exist.
Thus, a part of Africa I want to be, because a part of Africa I am.
It is the homeland--the place from which my ancestors came.
It is the homeland--a place which I will help to achieve success,
because, I am a part of Africa and shall forever be.

Our Struggle Against Drug Abuse

Our bodies we must not continue to abuse
with drugs and alcohol which we often misuse.
Because to our bodies we are inflicting great harm,
to the health-related community it is causing alarm.
Alcoholics and drug addicts, our hospitals fill,
many of whom cannot pay the bill.
They are detriments to the community in so many ways.
Expensive is the bill which society pays.
The economy suffers because of work hours that are lost.
Taxpayers are disturbed because of the escalating cost.

To support their habits many crimes, addicts commit.
Into our society they find it difficult to fit.
To their families they inflict unnecessary pain.
Often the spouses cannot stand the strain.
A child born of an addict may have a birth defect.
Many who are born healthy suffer from child neglect.
The addicts are victims of their own drug abuse.
Their once good minds become of no use.
From family and friends they suffer rejection.
Seldom is there a place where they can find affection.
So the abuse of drugs affects us all.
It threatens to bring about society's downfall.
What can we do to curtail this abuse?
More we must offer than just another excuse.
Let us tackle the problem before too late.
This, our duty, we cannot abdicate.
With both sellers and users we must effectively deal,
    before this sick society we can finally heal.
Drug abuse we may not be able to end,
    but in the struggle against it, our support we must lend.
All efforts are needed in this tremendous fight.
We must erase from society this terrible plight.

Our World of Tomorrow

Although the tomorrow of yesterday
    has now become today,
    my thoughts still are colored by events
    of the past.
I still view the world as I knew it and as I want it to be.
In seeing the world from my earlier perspective,
I became dismayed over what the future holds.
Then it occurred to me,
    that at all stages of my life, I have found myself

at odds with the world around me;
yet, I have always been able to survive.
Yes, the world of tomorrow will be quite different
from the one that I have known,
but somehow, I will rise to meet the challenge.
Boldly, I will insist that the world of tomorrow is as
much mine as that of any other inhabitant of the earth.
It will be affected by my fears, hopes, and aspirations.
I will help to decide the affairs of state,
because it is both my right and duty.
I will feel free to express my opinion loudly and clearly.
I, too, will live in the world of tomorrow.
These were good thoughts,
but I realize that the world in which I am living is real,
and while I am determined to stand my ground,
there are others around me who are even more adamant.
They are not demanding a voice in running the world
of tomorrow,
they are proclaiming themselves as the only voice.
Thus, our world will remain one in which some continue
to struggle to exert influence,
while others aggressively fight to pursue their dreams.
And so, the "tomorrow" of yesterday has become the "today."
It is not exactly what we had anticipated,
yet, it is the one in which we must live.

Parents in Search for Success

What roles do we play in the training of our children?
Do we share with them our love and care?
Appropriate discipline do we administer?
For adulthood are they being prepared?
A major role each parent must play,

since the training of the child on us depends.
While the church and schools share in the training,
the paramount duty belongs to the parents.
Love and understanding we must always provide them,
for the assurance of parents each child needs to know.
Our children we love, but they must be trained
because their lives beyond us they will have to live.
To our children, close friends we should be
but that doesn't mean that to them we must cater.
Appropriate discipline, parents should administer,
if love and respect are to be obtained.
Our children to us are very precious;
therefore, for their future we must carefully plan.
In their best interest we should always act,
even if at times our efforts they reject.
By their actions we should not be disturbed,
for mature judgment they are yet to possess.
Obtaining popularity should not be our goal,
but to gain their admiration in years ahead.
If we seek their love by to them kowtowing,
in later years resentment they may hold.
It is our obligation to train our children
to be responsible during their adult years.
This may mean designing a code of behavior,
and from its standards very seldom straying.
Appropriate guidance we must provide them--
being rigid when needed but with understanding.
Therefore, if our children we properly train,
respect for us they most likely will show.
And in later years we will not regret, that in our roles as parents we did not fail.

Passing the Torch

To the young the torch must be passed.
From our shoulders the burden must fall.
Therefore, the eagerness of the young
    to accept the challenge must be combined
    with our readiness to pass the torch.
Tired we are from years of struggle,
    and although willing to exercise leadership,
    our desire is not matched by our ability to perform.
Therefore, why do we resist the changing of the guard?
Why do we insist upon being captain of the ship
    when we lack the vision to guide it out of danger?
Are we mindful of our weaknesses,
    and how they are thwarting needed progress?
Are we aware that waiting in the wings
    are those who can offer us more challenging
    leadership?
Why are we denying them their opportunities?
Why are we guaranteeing disaster,
    by giving ineffective leadership
    to demanding causes?
The handwriting is on the wall,
    and to it we must respond.
The torch awaits new leadership,
    and to the young it must be given.
From the past, with dignity, we have brought it,
    but into the future, in new hands, it must go.

Prepare for the Transition

Into the Twenty-First Century we now have moved.
Was preparation for it adequately made?
With advancing technology are we able to cope?
If not, into the past we are bound to fade.
Fair warnings we received about what to expect;
    thus, adequate was the time for transition.
Did we choose, instead, to sit idle,
    and criticize those with greater ambition?
The world in which for long we lived,
    competent we were with our various interactions.
But the world of tomorrow, with its many innovations
    may cause for us major dissatisfactions.
We, who have always been so independent,
    now for our survival must on others depend.
Let this not be a reason to reject what is modern,
    for its many benefits will to us extend.
For this Twenty-First Century are we ready
    and farewell prepared to bid to the old?
On memories of the past we shall frequently reflect,
    now that a new century has begun to unfold.

Preserver of the Peace

Created it was as a preserver of peace,
    which was designed to serve humankind.
After World War II when the UN was formed,
    historic hatred it sought to leave behind.
Faith it expresses in basic human rights,
    and for social progress it also aims.
The practice of tolerance it strongly endorses,
    and strength through unity the Charter proclaims.
Mediation it uses to resolve conflicts--
    always utilizing its best envoys.

But when efforts fail to keep the peace,
a military force the UN deploys.
International warfare it tries to terminate,
and civil conflicts it seeks to end.
They threaten the lives of millions who are innocent.
who on the United Nations have begun to depend.
Concern it shows for raising health standards,
and world wide illiteracy it tries to erase.
Accommodation it provides for fleeing refugees,
and the political oppressed it seeks to embrace.
Colonial people it guides to nationhood,
and food for the hungry it often provides.
Actively, it has fought for social justice
for economic development it offers guides.
Yet, nations are still engaged in warfare,
and hungry children continue to cry.
Social justice is yet to be achieved;
therefore, the oppressed demand to know why.
Tremendous will be the task of the United Nations
in its endeavor to establish peace.
Now that we live in the 21st Century,
hopefully its efforts will not cease.

Prevailing Winds of Peace

Will the winds of peace ever blow our way,
bringing to us the tranquillity that long we have sought?
Will our hearts ever beat with true contentment,
realizing that, at last, with ourselves we are at peace?
The securing of peace involves a major undertaking,
since with our inner strife we must first contend.
Long and difficult will be this assignment,
for involved in a conflict are the body and soul.
While the spiritual being actively pursues peace,
the body usually displays a mood that is rebellious.

And too often, it is the cooperative spirit
that will yield to the body that is full of greed.
So we are involved in a tremendous struggle
to determine which course we shall pursue.
The inner conflict cannot be endless,
since on its outcome external peace depends.
Just as individuals are motivated by greed,
so are the nations which they lead.
Envy and pride are companion menaces,
that can provoke nations to needless hostility.
Peaceful persons, on the other hand, are very diplomatic.
They willingly champion the causes of peace.
Therefore, if they exist in significant numbers,
war-like attitudes we soon can end.
When our spiritual selves are victorious
and expel such vices as greed, envy and pride,
at peace with ourselves we shall become,
and a tranquil environment then create.
For at the root of peaceful existence is the individual,
whose lone voice can lead to a chorus
crying out for peace.
And since peaceful people make peaceful nations,
we can bring into existence a harmonious world.
Yes, the winds of peace can blow our way,
if the proper stimulation we willingly provide.
A meaningful step taken by just one person
can produce the lead that millions will follow.
Therefore, the winds of peace can blow our way,
and those winds can be prevailing.

Reacting to Raging Storms

Often there must be a raging storm,
    before we initiate much needed reform.
We wait for the crisis to get out of hand
    before we are willing to take command.
When we realize that it is too late
    the problem, then, we seek to abate.
Since solutions then will be in vain,
    there is nothing to do but suffer the pain.
For future crises we must prepare,
    they will happen, although sometimes rare.
If from day to day we evaluate,
    future problems, then, we can anticipate.
When there are signs of pending disaster,
    we can take steps the problems to master.
Then the raging storm we need not face,
    but only smaller problems will we have to erase.
What is to be gained when we procrastinate?
Do our responsibilities we abdicate?
What is achieved by our constant excuse?
Our failure to act is really an abuse.
We must not wait for the raging storm,
    before launching the much needed reform.

Reality

In a dream world at times we can live,
    but reality we must eventually face.
From above the clouds we must come down,
    and the truth about life begin to embrace.
Achievements are not given on golden platters;
    instead, for them we must toil.
Because others the same goals seek,
    in a fierce struggle we become embroil.

Fair is not every competition.
By lower standards some games are played.
Competitors are not always persons of character.
Morals of some will leave you dismayed.
By cheaters you will be confronted.
Their only interest is to win.
They boast not about their virtues.
No guilt they feel deep within.
Bias judges in making their decisions,
often rules of fairness lay aside.
To offers of bribery they don't say "no."
since money received help them to decide.
In a world of immorality decisions are made.
On corruption, only a few will frown.
If you fail to stoop to their low level,
the public will approve your "turn down."
Therefore, be realistic in playing the game,
for against an unfair breed you must compete.
If you have not proven that you are the best,
by the lesser qualified you will suffer defeat.
You are only dreaming about a world of fairness.
Such a world does not exist.
Fully prepare yourself to meet the challenge,
but surrender of your morals always resist.

Reawakening

This is a time of reawakening.
New life within us we must instill.
Dead we seem, although still breathing,
With new energy we must refill.
Why from the active are we disappearing?
Why at this time are we fast asleep?
Since promising are our many opportunities.
Now is the time to launch into the deep.

If in the race we fall behind,
our competitor will continue to move.
Greater will become the gap between us.
Making it difficult for us to improve.
Let us concentrate now on reawakening.
Over our situation let us pause and reflect.
If means we find for reinvigoration,
over our lives we'll have a greater effect.
Let this be our call to action.
From our costly sleep we must awake.
Our creative minds we must rapidly employ,
and innovative pursuits undertake.
Among the sleep we must not be found.
for great are the opportunities in which to engage.
Awake! we must be to accept the challenge,
and competitive must be each battle we wage.

Reliance on Government

In this nation we do believe, and on its government we rely.
For as weak individuals, we gain strength
when government with us allies.
Our weakness increases our reliance on government.
We need it to protect us from those enemies who intentionally,
or unintentionally seek to weaken or destroy us.
Since we are lacking in capital we cannot stand toe to toe with
the controllers of wealth and wielders of power.
We seek an ally in government,
not to provide for our needs, but to support just causes.
It is argued that we can determine the course of government
through our votes,
but that does not always accord with reality.
Too often limited choices are given to us
by those who manipulate the nominating process.

Therefore, even though our nation is composed of political
equals, everyone does not carry the same political weight.
Politically, we are dwarfs
when compared with the giant campaign contributors.
Our lack of political clout results in diminished political returns.
Therefore, our helplessness makes a friendly government a
necessity, if we are to enjoy the fruits of our democracy.
Because our needs and expectations lead us to place
our full confidence in government; it can deceive us.
No longer should we be pawns in its political games.
We want our government to be an institution of trust
rather than the source of our many frustrations.
At a time when it seems as if our enemies are numerous,
we do not want to feel that our government is conniving with
them to undermine or destroy us.
We need a government that is composed of role models,
who will inspire us to achieve our best;
rather than political leaders who will surrender to corruption,
and make decisions that will only further their political
gains.
We do not need leaders who, by their contemptible actions
succeed in bringing the nation to shame.
We want a government in which the weak can identify--
one which can promote our interest.
We want a government that will instill within us a sense of pride
and invoke within us a feeling of full patriotism.
We want a government in which we can be proud.

Restraining the Oppressors

Who is there to give hope to the hopeless,
by being the voice who for them will speak?
Who is there to restrain the oppressors,
and bring comfort to those who are weak?

Loud is the voice of the possessors of wealth,
whose influence in government is far too strong.
Loyal support they receive from the public,
which criticizes them rarely, even when wrong.
People of all classes seem to laud them--
their accumulation of wealth we highly praise.
Since we give encouragement by our show of approval,
the status of humanity they don't seek to raise.
Somehow, our system we will have to change,
if a just society is ever to prevail.
The cause of the weak we must begin to champion,
if not democracy is sure to fail.
We must expose those, who are engaged in oppression,
while casting our lot with those who are poor.
Society must frown on all forms of injustice,
by opening for the downtrodden, opportunity's door.

Retreat Not from Progress

The hands of time we cannot turn backward,
reversing gains which we have made.
Because progress for us has often been difficult,
into the past we cannot let it fade.
Improvements we have made in scientific technology,
therefore, into a new age we all have been swept.
Numerous are the problems introduced by innovation,
which if ignored will make us seem inept.
To modern change we have been affected;
therefore, to it we will have to react.
Throughout history, adjustments have been made,
with only the very sacred remaining in tact.
Because it is to the presence that we must respond
only minor consideration we need give to the past.
Being aware of it will help us to make wise decisions,
but on future endeavors our eyes we must cast.

Good might have been the cherished days of old,
    but never again to them can we return.
A part of our memory they will always be,
    but for a brighter tomorrow our hearts should yearn.
In a world of change we must always move forward,
    and not into complacency ever retreat.
We must adjust our lives to modern innovation,
    and never by them allow defeat.

Road to Somewhere

Travel the road that leads to somewhere.
Waste not time on a dead end street.
Plot well your course and follow it,
    and the future you will be ready to greet.
Follow the road that leads to somewhere.
Never mind the heckling crowd.
If you continue to pursue your course,
    of yourself you will feel very proud.
If the highway, at times, is congested,
    an alternate route you, then, should take.
But lose not sight of where you are going,
    if a successful journey you are to make.
Sometimes the road is fraught with danger--
    of the detours be fully aware.
Slow your speed when it is needed;
    in times of trouble you must drive with care.
If you travel the road that leads to nowhere,
    misfortune will be your eventual fate.
You will have to make up for time you've wasted;
    therefore, achieving your goal may be too late.
In life you must travel the proper highway,
    if success you expect to obtain.
Plot your course and effectively pursue it,
    then, peace and happiness will be your gain.

Roles of Tradition

Never should we be dominated by traditions,
although in our lives they have a place.
A sense of continuity they often provide us,
but not all customs should we embrace.
Traditions that are useful we should accommodate,
because needed strength they will enable us to gain.
A sense of stability they will give us;
therefore, those that are practical we should retain.
Be not hasty in discarding traditions--
those that are productive should still be used.
Some may need drastic modification;
thus, with innovative ideas they should be infused.
Because some traditions are rich in meaning;
they have survived for many years.
They have been employed in new situations,
and they have helped to relieve our inmost fears.
Some traditions are totally useless,
but deference to them we continue to pay.
They prevent us from making necessary progress,
by imposing too many obstacles in our way.
We must assess carefully our various traditions,
and determine which we should continue to use.
Those that are practical we can retain,
but to consider them all sacred is no excuse.
Let not tradition for us be a burden,
which we feel we must observe.
With great haste, let us dispose of those,
which no longer a purpose serve.
Over traditions, we must be masters;
their servants we must never be.
If better use we make of them,
we can be restricted while remaining free.

Scars of the Past

Scars of the past are long lasting.
It seems as if they never heal.
Because in later years, they will cause new eruptions,
    their damaging impact we cannot conceal.
Events of the past are not easily forgotten,
    even if to forget them we make a vow.
To later problems they are often related;
    therefore, to the past we must constantly bow.
On pages of history past events are recorded;
    which keep old issues partially awake.
Temporarily, they seem as if forgotten,
    but they wait to influence any decision we make.
Enemies made many years ago,
    may resurface when we least expect.
If we plan our strategy with that in mind,
    on our efforts they'll have minimal effect.
Old wounds, too often, are reopened,
    revealing dark secrets known only to a few.
Bitter then becomes the struggle,
    as conflicts of the past appear anew.
We must try seriously to put the past behind us,
    and leave no scars that long will last.
Then, less complicated will be our endeavors,
    since linked they are not with efforts of the past.
If when victorious we are gentle,
    those whom we opposed will soon forgive.
This can put past conflicts behind us;
    therefore, giving animosity little chance to live.

Search for Solutions

Today, we are in search of a problem solver--
    one who extraordinary talent possesses,
    one who can, first, initiate new ideas,
    then mold them effectively into successes.
We need persons who can design programs,
    that will fortify us against violent crime.
Not temporary protection that will not last,
    but a fortress built that will endure through time.
How can we solve the problems of poverty?
Are you one with a unique dream?
Can it be transformed into reality,
    if we work together as a team?
Racism for us remains a problem,
    which often results from a distorted mind.
With serious thoughts and creativity,
    a workable solution, perhaps, we will find.
Our environment we continue to abuse,
    because practical solutions are difficult to obtain.
For perceptive ideas we constantly search,
    in order that abuses we can restrain.
In our society there are many challenges,
    and responses to them we must make.
Let us encourage our dreamers and thinkers
    and of their creative ideas willingly partake.

Secure at Home?

All around us are scenes of violence.
Even in our homes we cannot feel secure.
Nervously, we lie awake at night,
    fearing that intruders might our sleep disturb.
In our homes we often are prisoners,
    looking out at a violent world.

Burglar bars we have for our safety,
    making our homes seem like prisoners' cells.
With high fences we surround ourselves,
    and with security devices of every kind.
Fierce dogs we have for further protection,
    and even with these we are still afraid.
To visitors, our homes were once beacons,
    welcoming everyone to visit there.
Today, a telephone call is needed;
    therefore, if you do not call do not appear.
Our outside activities are severely limited,
    as inside we are forced to stay.
Even there we have no safety,
    for house invaders we have to fear.
Into the streets we dare not venture,
    because too much violence there we will find.
Our evening activities we often limit;
    under house arrest, too often, we are found.
How can our houses become homes again?
When can we enjoy them and feel at ease?
When full security will we ever know?
Our homes we must make a true place to live.

Selfish Pursuits

Too often into the heavens we look
    when to greater height we seek to ascend.
Only with our goals do we become concerned,
    caring little about those whom we offend.
Those around us we willingly abuse
    in order our goals to obtain.
The best for ourselves we seek to achieve,
    even though upon others we inflict great pain.
Why do we pretend to be humanitarians,
    and in the interest of others are motivated to act;

when in essence our motives are selfish,
and sometimes with Satan we have a pact.
Not forever can we disguise
the hidden motives which we possess.
Eventually will come the day of reckoning
and with it the end of our success.
So let us build on solid foundations,
and with the highest ethics our goals pursue.
Aiming always to be successful,
but giving to others respect that is due.
We must never upon another trod
in order our goals to achieve.
If forever we strive with fairness,
rich will be the blessings which we receive.

Show Me Evidence

Show me evidence of your commitment
to the cause you made your aim.
Have you sacrificed your time and effort
in order to obtain the goal you claim?
To the cause are you truly committed?
Are you contributing to the cause?

Show me evidence of your leadership
in waging a campaign to achieve your dream.
Have you attained a creditable record
of inspiring the members of your team?
To the cause have you demonstrated leadership?
Are you giving leadership to this noble cause?

Show me evidence of your endurance
in pursuing this cause until the end.
Have you been able to encounter the hardships
and against such obstacles refuse to bend?
For the cause will you endure?
Are you enduring in pursuit of your cause?

Show me evidence of your unfailing courage
when against the opposition you must stand.
Have you confronted them without retreating,
remaining steadfast in your demand?
For the cause have you demonstrated courage?
Are you showing courage in pursuit of your cause?

A commitment is needed to obtain your objective;
therefore, dedicated leadership you must provide.
You must endure in spite of the hardships,
and with unfailing courage stem the tide.
Have you leadership and commitment?
With unfailing courage can you endure?

Solid Foundation

As a child with good parents I was blessed,
who taught me the difference between right and wrong.
With a loving extended family I was reinforced,
everyone working together helped to make me strong.
My little rural school taught me sound values,
while my family's church brought me inspiration.
The elders of the community sought to encourage me.
All helped me to form a Christian foundation.
Songs that I sang provided me strength.

Books which I read gave me reasons to aspire.
My radio allowed me a broader world to experience.
What greater enrichment could I ever desire?
Therefore, as a child on this foundation I built,
    which allowed me, at last, adulthood to reach
From the experiences of my childhood years,
    lessons of value I will be able to teach..
Throughout my life I have achieved many triumphs,
    yet, there have been times when I have known defeat.
But because of my background which God provided,
    from my Christian commitments I will not retreat.

Solutions are Within Our Reach

How long will our problems defy solutions,
    when appropriate answers are within our reach?
Are we lacking in courage to resolve them,
    merely because of consequences we will have to face?
What price will we pay for this procrastination?
Will it be more costly than the consequences of action?
Why then are we refusing to address these problems?
Why are we insisting on this prolonged delay?
Our failure to confront societal problems and resolve them,
    cannot be attributed to the lack of solutions
    especially, when many of the answers are very clear.
Many promising solutions we have never considered,
    since vested interest we have sought to protect.
Addressing critical problems relative to poverty, race relations,
    and the environment will mean challenging the status quo,
    and this we are not prepared to do.
We choose instead, to pursue policies in which the losers
    will continue to lose; therefore, we are pushed closer to the brink of national disaster. In a democratic society, why does the majority act cowardly,
    when it is within its power to make the necessary reforms?

By our various actions, both economically and politically,
we, too often, condone the very policies we claim to oppose.
We support approaches which add power to those
who possess power, which by implication,
makes the weak weaker.
Therefore, those seeking to bring about greater equity in society
have only slight chances of obtaining success.
The same is true with those seeking to bring about
true diversity within the nation,
and those trying to adopt meaningful policies
to conserve our environment.
In most cases, possessors of power
have much to gain by retaining the status quo.
Therefore, we continue to bemoan the critical problems
confronting this nation, and prophesy
as to the consequences to which they will lead.
Commissions we will form to find solutions,
when answers exist within our reach.
We are not blind to what is required,
but we lack the courage of implementation.

Spending a Day With Children

If when with children we spend just a day,
our earlier years we can re-live.
As childhood memories we vividly recall,
for a return to youth, what will we give?
To the past, however, we cannot return--
only recollections of it can we behold.
On this special day, however, we can dream
of being children who are yet to grow old.
In their world if we live just one day,
and experience innovations which were to us unknown.
We can become familiar with the joys children feel,
and claim their problems as our very own.

From this encounter the children, too, will learn
    of the various problems with which seniors must cope.
Aware they will be of our rich experiences,
    while also recognizing our lack of hope.
So the children receive a view of the future,
    and as seniors, we revisit the past.
If only one day together we can spend,
    our memories of it for long will last.

Swimming Upstream

There are lofty goals which I seek.
These I can obtain while remaining meek.
There are mountain's highs to which I can rise,
And yet wanton powers not exercise.
There are beautiful dreams which I behold
Of how society we can remold.
Give me the chance to pursue my dream.
Encourage me while I swim upstream.

In my pathway, please, no obstacle place.
Rather help me difficulties to face.
Criticize me in a constructive way--
Offer me encouragement with words you say.
By working together we shall succeed.
Unity of effort is what we need.
Give me the chance to pursue my dream.
Assure me while I swim upstream.

Soon in the victory lane we will stand.
Over our destiny we'll have command.
In a just society we shall live.
Where trust and respect to each we'll give.
It is a better world that I perceive.
In its reality I do believe.

Give me the chance to pursue my dream.
Inspire me and I will swim upstream.

Teamwork

There are hardships that we must overcome,
which can be achieved if we work as a team.
If everyone could the burden share,
realize we will our long held dream.
Some things in life are easier accomplished,
when team efforts we employ.
If collectively we can win our struggle,
the fruits of our labor we all can enjoy.
Since as a community we continue to suffer,
as a unit we should respond.
If personal ambitions we put aside,
we can establish among us a common bond.
If with a proposal you disagree,
be not one to hold your hands.
Give the idea a chance to be tested,
before to the body you make demands.
Being tactful will promote unity,
for the teamwork which we need.
Therefore, if in all things we are diplomatic,
our campaign for justice can succeed.
We are involved in a serious endeavor--
one from which we must never retreat.
But if effective teamwork we do not exhibit,
doom are our efforts to sure defeat.

These Houses are Not Homes

There are many houses which still are standing,
although as homes they exist no more.

For gone are the families which gave them life,
    and unstable tenants reside there now.
In one of these houses a story tells
    of the struggle of a family as it came into being.
Each room in it has a historic meaning;
    therefore, for this family it was a home, indeed.
It was a place where family members gathered,
    who came from places both far and near.
It was a place of relaxation--
    a welcome retreat from a world of care.
It was a house which stood so stately.
Family members regarded it as a source of pride.
To the community it was a house of beauty.
Hospitality awaited you when you arrived.
Of little value now is that quaint old house,
    to the tenants, in transit, who there reside.
For them, it is only a temporary shelter;
    they never considered it as their home.
No interest they have in its maintenance.
They appear to be destructive in so many ways.
No love they have for their place of living,
    since it is not their home they just don't care.
What has happened to this grand old house,
    which once was as elegant as a house could be?
Where is the beauty it once embraced?
Why now the ugliness which we see?
Gone now is the family which lived there once,
    although its legacy will long remain.
No longer does it exemplify beauty,
    for it's only a house, it's not a home.

Tomorrow is an Extension of Today

A challenging tomorrow lies just ahead;
    therefore, for it we will need to prepare.

As a new experience it will be,
only in part, since it is an extension of today.
Our future is heavily depended on our current activities;
therefore, mistakes made today bring into existence
serious obstacles for tomorrow.
So let us not minimize the impact of our present performances
upon our future roles.
The goals which we will strive so hard to obtain tomorrow,
will be the results of our dreams of today.
And our ability to achieve them will depend upon the discipline
which we have already developed.
Our tomorrow will be only as effective as the preparation
we have made for it.
Therefore, we must act as if our tomorrow
will truly depend upon it.
The road we pave should be designed to facilitate our arrival there,
rather than create obstacles that will deter us from
the desircd goal.
Our past should present us with workable blue-prints
that will enable us to discard ideas that are unfeasible,
and encourage us to make improvements over previously
tried plans.
Our valuable lessons of the past and clear vision
should permit us to entertain realistic dreams
of what tomorrow can be.
And with the achievement or failure of our goals,
we will better understand that life is a single continuum--
where we move systematically from the past to the future.
Tomorrow will not be a new experience,
merely an extension of today.

Understudies

Under our wings we will guide them,
as we train them to be the very best.
Every detail we will teach them,
in preparation for the demanding test.
For this mission they were already groomed.
Proper discipline they had obtained.
With their mission they were familiar;
therefore, any thought of failure they disdain.
So good are our chances of training them
for challenging positions which they will hold.
Since effective leaders they are replacing,
their leadership must be creative and very bold.
We accept the challenge to prepare them properly,
since valuable are experiences which we possess.
Through our inputs we will maintain continuity,
and better prepare them for achieving success.
We are responsible to future generations;
therefore, leaders of tomorrow we must prepare.
Not to be carbon copies of us,
but extraordinary leaders who are very rare.
We accepted these as our understudies;
therefore, competent training they will receive.
For soon to them the torch will be passed,
and the challenge will be for them to achieve.

Uniting Our Efforts for Peace

United were the nations in search of peace,
as the Second World War neared its end.
Millions had sacrificed by giving their lives,
now it was time for broken ties to mend.
Small powers and large powers together formed
an organization called the United Nations.

A major aim was the preservation of peace
through the harmonizing of international relations.
Consideration it gave to how wars begin
in order to abort them at the earliest stage.
Methods of mediation it put in place
so that devastating wars we wouldn't have to wage.
Collective security was a plan devised
to oppose nations which pursue aggression.
An international force the UN will deploy
Rather than to aggressors make a concession
Peace with justice is a UN goal,
and universal human rights it also proclaims.
Social and economic problems it tries to resolve
and for self determination of people the organization aims.
Numerous have been the UN's achievements
in its efforts to obtain universal peace.
It has halted aggression of numerous nations,
causing war-like leaders their hostilities to cease.
Strides it has made in its fight against illiteracy,
and health standards it has been able to raise.
It has given refuge to millions in flight.
For its humanitarian efforts it deserves praise.
On the other hand, it has its share of problems,
which can be resolved when attitudes are changed.
Unfair is the representation in the Security Council,
thus, its membership needs to be rearranged.
Few heed the plea for the recruitment of troops,
and financial assessments usually go unpaid.
Many nations fail to honor their pledges,
causing too much of the burden on a few to be laid.
Sure, the UN has a number of weaknesses,
which it advocates should strive to amend.
But it is the world's best hope for survival,
so support for its efforts, let us extend.

Utilize Potentials

Recognize potentials within your midst,
which should never be allowed to go unused.
Challenge the skillful to become actively involved,
but their willingness never should be abused.
In many areas there are needs for servants,
but few who are talented are eager to serve.
Convince those who possess potentials,
that a commitment to service they should observe.
Sure they are likely to be reluctant,
contending that they cannot succeed.
They will tell you that they lack the time,
and that more experience they surely need.
Don't give in to their reluctance,
for the truly talented is difficult to find.
Recruit them as your understudies,
and let them work with the very best minds.
In every way give them encouragement--
creativity, let them employ.
Give them assignments that are very challenging,
and their work they will enjoy.
Allow them to utilize their innovations--
their new ideas do not reject.
Carefully guide them as they develop,
by showing to them your greatest respect.
These are persons with great potentials.
Creative minds they do possess.
Place no obstacles in their pathway.
Applaud them as they achieve success.
In them, we recognize true potentials.
To the mountain top they certainly can rise.
They will lead us to a better tomorrow,
for us they are our greatest prize.

Values We Instill

We are the molders of the next generation.
In them our hopes we expect to fulfill.
By our words and actions we seek to train them.
Our morals within them we endeavor to instill.
A curriculum we devise and expect them to follow,
  while cultural changes we disregard.
But if success we anticipate achieving,
  many rules of the past we will have to discard.
Children learn not only from designated plans,
  but from all in life that they observe.
Therefore, if our words match not our actions,
  from lessons taught them they soon will swerve.
How effective are the sermons we preach,
  when the lives we live much louder speak.
Overshadowed are the messages we send them,
  because the character we reflect is far too weak.
How bleak to us the future seems,
  because current morals we strongly detest.
We should question not how this came to be,
  since in faulty training we did invest.
If a better society we expect tomorrow,
  clearer we must be in the messages we send.
Thus, blame not others for leading our youths astray,
  until our faults in character we first amend.

Ventures

What menace will I conquer today?
What evil thought will I expel?
What battle must I continue to wage?
Against what practice must I rebel?
A major menace I will seek to conquer,
  and against violence I will take a stand.

Upon others I will not inflict it.
I will leave it to God to reprimand.
Thoughts of evil I must expel.
I cannot allow them to clog my mind.
For deeper thoughts I must allow to enter,
    if contentment I am ever to find.
A battle against intransigence I must wage.
    as challenging tasks I undertake.
Valuable time I cannot waste;
    therefore, patterns of laziness I must forsake.
Against practices of intolerance I must rebel
Never upon another should I frown.
Nor allow friends in my presence.
    a fellow-human ever to put down.
Yes, there are menaces which I can conquer,
    and there are evil thoughts which I must expel.
There are critical battles which I shall wage,
    and to my many bad practices I must rebel.

Very Few Possessions

On the front porch an old lady sits,
    reflecting on the days which long have gone.
Many pleasant memories she will never forget,
    since they are among her few possessions.
Soon from this house she will be taken,
    perhaps, to see it never again.
She sits and collects her pleasant memories,
    which are among her precious possessions.
Very little time she has for tears,
    for too many, in her life have fallen.
Numerous obstacles she has overcome,
    but real strength she will need to face tomorrow.
In loneliness now on her porch she waits,
    even though others are by her side.

They know not means by which to console her,
for in her world of depression they do not abide.
What will be this old lady's fate?
In happiness, again, will she ever live?
Will life for her now be a waiting period,
as departed loved ones she prepares to see?
Good by, she has said to her past lifestyle--
one that was rich in so many ways.
In relative luxury she once lived,
but few are the things which she now possesses.

The time now has come and gone,
but still on the porch she quietly waits.
Although another hour she has been given;
it is not a reprieve from her pending disaster.
As a tragedy this story will end,
when from her home she leaves forever.
A few more years, perhaps, she will live,
with cherished memories as her only possession.

Violence

Violence in society we must curtail.
Against this evil let us wage a fight.
Best known strategies we must employ,
and with dedication end this blight.
The reduction of violence will not be easy,
since in society it has established a place.
Factors which underlie it we must examine
before the problem, itself, we seriously face.
We must increase our use of mediation,
at every level where there is friction--
family, community, state and nation,
and the international arena, in addition.

If we better seek to understand each other,
    many conflicts would cease to exist;
But if others around us we take advantage,
    attitudes of violence are likely to persist.
Must we continue to employ violence?
Is there a more sensible way in which to live?
Violence we can reduce by far,
    if more often we are willing to forgive.
If forgiving attitudes begin in the family,
    and then to the next level quickly move,
    these attitudes can penetrate all levels of society,
    then, our chances for coexistence will improve.
Let me reduce my level of violence,
    then, encourage others, likewise to act.
If everyone will be a little less violent,
    the reduction of violence will be a fact.

Voices

A voice is needed which can be heard--
    one that is willing to challenge the wrong.
A voice that seldom will be silent--
    one that when necessary will be strong.
A voice is needed to condemn intolerance,
    and that will admonish us not to hate.
A voice that will teach us to live together,
    and that to each other try to relate.
A voice is needed to appeal for justice,
    especially for those who are very poor.
Not for the rich only, does justice belong.
For the oppressed we must open the door.
A voice we need to speak out for peace.
Methods of resolving conflicts it can suggest.
Mediation should be a preferred method.
A world of tranquillity is our major quest.

A voice is needed to deplore poverty,
    and a war against greed eventually wage.
Hopefully, millions will join the campaign,
    and move humanity to a higher stage.
I want to have a powerful voice,
    which for worthy causes will loudly speak.
I want to be able to bring about change,
    and better the lives of those who are weak.

Volunteerism

Numerous are the tasks which must be done,
    but few are those who will volunteer.
Limited funds are available for improvement,
    but from critical needs we cannot veer.
For necessities we must often depend
    on volunteers who are willing to serve.
Skills in abundance we possess;
    therefore, why from service do we swerve.
Volunteers are needed in the fight against poverty.
Many things we can do to assist the poor.
Hunger and homelessness we can help alleviate.
For those who are deprived we can open the door.
Your ability to create, why not use
    to help society its many problems remove?
If a few hours of creativity you can provide,
    so many things around us we can improve.
Why not to the challenge respond today,
    by volunteering for some task to perform--
A task that will humanity enhance,
    and in some way help to raise the norm.
Must all of our services be rendered for pay?
Aren't there contributions to life which we can make?
Since what we possess was by God's blessings,
    why not let society of our service partake?

When Your Word is Given

When your word is given it should be like gold.
We depend on you for it to uphold.
From it, you should never turn away.
Once it is uttered it should be here to stay.
A commitment when made, you should observe,
    and not seek ways from it to swerve.
On you, others should be able to depend;
    therefore, be cautious about the message you send.
Be specific when to others you speak.
Commitments you make should not be weak.
Words with double meaning hesitate to use.
Speak not big words in order to confuse.
When in doubt about what you hear,
    do not react until it is clear.
Thus, when your commitment is finally made,
    its observance let no one dissuade.
Cause not others to experience defeat,
    because of obligations you did not meet.
Promise not what you cannot give,
    for once it is spoken, long should it live.
Let the assurance you give form a special bond.
Consider it as precious and of it be fond.
Let not your words into the wind be blown,
    for by your speech and action, you are defined and known.

Where the Wind Blows

Somewhere there is a land where the wind blows,
    and even though we are overwhelmed by the heat of summer,
    we are constantly refreshed by the gentle breeze.
The blowing wind and rushing sea seem to say to me:
    "welcome, this land is yours.

See the sand on which your father walked.
See the water that bathed his weary feet.
See the trees which are products of the ones that provided
comforting shade as he walked along the beach.
See the land that once was the home of your father.
See the land that belongs to you."
So after years of dreaming about the homeland,
at last, I have come to the land which my father knew.
I, too, have come to feel the gentle breeze,
to cool myself in the shade of the island's trees,
and to bathe my feet in the flowing water.
I have come to partake of fruits which I longed to taste.
I know that it was business that brought me here,
and that there are people whom I must see,
but those things can wait.
Today, I want to be a part of nature.
I want to see the sea with its many colors,
that tells from whence the water has come
and where it must go again.
I want to watch the leaves of the coconut trees,
as they react to the advancing wind--
fighting constantly and never standing still.
As I observe this struggle to survive,
my thoughts returned to the land from whence I came--
a land where trees are not forever at war against the blowing
wind.
But the trees of the islands tell a story of people,
who, like the trees I see, must constantly struggle for
survival,
and can never be totally free.
Yes, this is the land of my father,
and my presence here brings me joy.
I gain great pleasure from what I see,
and dream dreams of what it can be.
Trees here yielded shade for my father,
and today, they provide shade to comfort me.

Yes, I will rest well tonight, I know,
for in this land the wind still blows.

Why

Why do we dwell on things of the past,
which only cause our troubles to last?
Why not turn another page,
and move on to a higher stage?
Why be controlled by things gone by,
when the situation we can rectify?
Why must we endure internal strife,
when we can pursue a better life?
Why must we always live under a cloud,
when we can do something in which to be proud?
Why can't we, good decisions make,
and then proceed, effective action take?
Why aren't we willing to bring about change,
and control those things within our range?
Why not the problem eliminate,
instead of being contented to procrastinate?
Why are we not doers of good deeds,
who constantly sow productive seeds?
Why not kindness to others show,
and allow true love from us to flow?
Why not hostility with neighbors vacate,
by employing love rather than hate?
Why of ourselves don't we freely give,
so in peace with others we can truly live?

Why the Alienation

With society they are alienated,
only hypocrisy do they see.

Words which for so long they have read
are inconsistent with what exists.
With universal rights they are familiar,
because the Declaration they have often read;
Yet around them there is mass starvation
and political persecution almost everywhere.
Where can one find peace and justice?
For the oppressed, does anyone care?
Beautiful are our international documents,
but implementation is just not there.
From our political system they are alienated.
Hypocrisy exists virtually everywhere.
Politicians promise us everything we want,
but after election they just don't care.
Corruption in government is a normal practice,
which in high places we have grown to expect.
But not in politics is it limited,
for throughout society it is usually found.
So proudly we speak of constitutional rights,
and the equality for all which is there proclaimed,
but in our society we find no justice.
The implementation is just not there.
We question, why are they alienated,
when by their actions they can bring about change.
We don't understand that they are frustrated,
because in constant efforts they have always failed.
We consider them to be idealistic,
when action not words they usually demand.
We accuse them of being naive,
when our hypocrisy they disdain.
How can we curtail the growing alienation,
which cripples society in too many ways?
Cannot we match our words with action?
It is implementation that must be there.

With Our Riches

Although short may be our journey through life,
    on the many lives around us we can exert an effect.
With our God-given wealth we can make a difference
    by helping the "least among us" to gain respect.
Enriched we are in order others to enrich.
Our received blessings are for us to share.
Because bountifully has been our harvest of riches,
    for the world around us we should show our care.
Rich we may not be in earthly possessions,
    but almost everyone has something to give.
Even one small act of timely kindness,
    may give one who is struggling the strength to live.
When early in life we are taught the joy of giving,
    experience of worthiness we can constantly partake.
We can feel that humanity we are helping to enhance
    by the contributions of value which to it we make.
If investments in life we make daily
Feelings of reward we are sure to feel.
Not only from earth's riches would we have partaken,
    but the wounds of the oppressed we would have helped
    to heal.

Xenophobia

Why foreigners do we reject,
    before by us they are adequately known?
Why other cultures we consider inferior,
    thinking none is worthy but our own?
When other countries we chance to visit,
    why their cultures do we "put down"?
Do we attempt to learn their languages,
    or on anything but English do we frown?
How valuable do we consider our money?

Can it for our rudeness pay?
Do we feel that in impoverished countries,
    with a show of dollars we can have our way?
We perceive their governments as being puppets.
On their leaders we look with disdain.
When they do not heed our many demands,
    to the American government we quickly complain.
Foreigners we often despise,
    even when we are tourists in their land.
Sometimes I think that we visit other countries,
    merely to show that we are in command.
Sooner or later, we will be unwelcome strangers
    and hatred from others we are sure to receive.
But because others we too often mistreated,
    over our misfortune there will be few to grieve.

Yesterdays of My Life

The yesterday of my life has gone forever,
    but from my memory it will never fade.
Its many triumphs I shall remember,
    but I long to forget the mistakes I've made.
Not a single incident can I erase,
    for in my memory they are permanently stored.
Very minimal are their impact,
    but never can they be ignored.
What I am, and shall ever become
    from the past received its start.
Achievements were from good seed sown,
    and good fruits they will for long impart.
Failures in life also came from the past--
    from mistake which I will long regret.
The scars are there to forever remind me,
    and the impact I shall never forget.
To correct the past we can do in part,

and sometimes a better life live.
From the experiences which we encountered,
advice to others we can freely give.
We must treat yesteryears with great respect,
and from them never try to hide.
For the past is the basis for our today;
therefore, it should be treated as a useful guide.

Youths in an Age of Confusion

In this age characterized by confusion,
the young man sought to wrestle with the world around him.
There was so much expected of those who must rise to manhood,
yet there was too much trivia associated with the childhood
from which he sought to escape.
It was this duality that seemed to have overwhelmed him.
In order to prove that he was yet a child required only humility,
and deference to his elders,
but to proclaim that he had grown to manhood demanded
much more.
There were many tests which had to be taken,
and numerous initiations to endure.
To be a man, they said, he had to acquire the ability
to smoke cigarettes effectively,
to use profanity in a "professional" manner,
to consume enough alcohol
to become thoroughly intoxicated,
to experiment with drugs of various types,
and to seduce a woman or two, then brag.
All of these were characteristics associated with the induction
into manhood.
Sitting there, confused over his current status,
the look of relative innocence reflected on his face.
Perhaps, he, too, sought the answer to Shakespeare's question:
"to be or not to be."

It was obvious that what he felt that he had to do,
was not at all what he wanted to do.
Instead of defining himself, he appeared willing
to let others assume that responsibility.
He did not do what he wanted to do,
but did what his peers decided
that he had to do in order
to be considered worthy of entering into
manhood, as they defined it.
As he talked, the duality became more pronounced.
He seemed to have realized that even to seek advice was a childish act;
therefore, as a man his questions had to be made into statements
which could evoke the sought-after responses.
He felt compelled to disagree strongly with his own beliefs,
in order to prove manhood.
As I listened to the young man,
I thought about the difficult ritual involved in the passage
from boyhood to manhood.
Suddenly, it occurred to me that in some African countries,
boys passed ceremonially into manhood.
Since this was done on a group basis,
it did not force one to act out of character
in order to demonstrate to the satisfaction of others
that at last he had ceased to be a boy and now was a man.
As our conversation progressed,
it was clear that I, too, had become a major actor in the drama.
I was not viewing the young man as he was,
but seeing him as I wanted him to be.
Errors of judgment were minimized, and good intentions were
emphasized rather than his unbecoming behavior.
Suddenly, I could understand the goals he sought--
the desires he held, and the tasks he thought he had to undertake.

My sympathetic understanding, however,
did not bring easy solutions to his problems.
His greatest weakness appeared to have been his inability
to come to grips with the problems he faced,
to analyze them thoroughly and dispose of them.
On the other hand, his strongest point was his courage to question--
even though in a mild manner--
to challenge those things which he did not believe,
to reject accepted practices which he found to be repulsive to his taste.
Again and again, the duality of boyhood and manhood pervaded the scene,
as he spoke of the constant problems which were besetting him.
To be young in a world of the old gives one a dreadful feeling,
but, perhaps, worse is to be old in a world that is young.
In the world in which he lived,
it was difficult to do what appeared to be the right or
decent thing when all around him was rebelling, and the
last resemblance of order seemed to have been replaced
by chaos.
The world which the young man had dreams of building
was one which could stand the test of time,
but it was at a time when all else appeared
to be tentative, and built on shifting sand.
Even though he knew it, and I knew it even better,
the world which he envisioned was not yet to be.

Bridges

Are you willing to be a bridge
and bring together opposing sides?

Can you be that unifying force
    to hold us together against raging tides?
Can you cure the disease of hatred
    that is tearing our world asunder?
Will you lead a moral crusade
    to correct forever the initial blunder?

Are you willing to be a bridge,
    and bring together the young and old?
Are there proposals which you can offer--
    recommendations that are unique and bold?
Can all classes in unison work,
    a better nation in order to make?
If together you can bring us,
    then, of fruits of progress we all can partake.

Are you willing to be a bridge
    and people of all races together bring?
Can you develop an imaginative scheme
    that from racial hatred will remove the sting?
Can various religions be brought together
    for the good of humanity jointly to strive?
Can you be that special bridge
    that will enable peace forever to thrive?

Courage as a Weapon

Fear brings about your conquest;
Therefore, to it never surrender.

Maintain always a high level of courage.
Needed strength it will engender.
From some problems you can not run;
Therefore, you must be prepared to fight.
From somewhere then, you must summon courage
That will transform your weakness into might.
Courage can convince your most determined foe
To cease harassing and flee in fright.
If your hidden weakness cannot be detected.
A hero you will be, who was willing to fight.
Courage builds on acts of courage.
Dismissing from one all traces of fear.
If cowardly thoughts you never think,
When courage is needed it will appear.
Courage gives one an optimistic outlook;
Therefore, lessening the chances for defeat.
Even when faced with superior forces,
Because of your courage you will be hard to beat.
Make courage always your basic weapon.
Against it very few will dare to stand.
Your rights then, you can always protect,
Because over your destiny you have command.

Feeling Rewarded

I want to feel rewarded,
For some challenge which I have met.

I want to address an urgent problem,
Which others chose to forget.
I want to feel good each day,
Believing that I have done some worthy deeds.
I would like to learn in later years
That I helped to sow productive seeds.
I want to feel a sense of triumph,
Knowing that I have conquered greed.
Being aware that I have willingly given
To efforts which helped another succeed.
I want to feel that I still can contribute
To the many good causes which remain.
I want to be able to continue to labor
And know that my work will not be in vain.
Yes, I want to feel rewarded
As new objectives I seek to fulfill.
Perhaps, contributions which I am able to make
May a brighter vision in others instill.

Freedom

Throughout the world people cry for freedom.
No one in slavery is contented to be.
For years they have struggled for liberation.
Like the birds of the wilds they want to be free.
Too often, in captivity they are held
By those who for their freedom have fought.
Although loudly proclaiming its virtues,
Freedom for others was never their thought.
Hypocrisy, we will have to defeat,
Before liberation for all we can obtain
The blessing of freedom opponents should know,

Since their own liberation they had to gain.
During the last half of the twentieth century,
For world wide freedom we have aimed.
International conferences have frequently endorsed it
And by the United Nations it is often proclaimed.
Such dreams, however, are far from reality.
Throughout the world for them we fight.
Helpless the world seems to be
In alleviating the downtrodden's plight.
All people deserve a taste of freedom,
And control of their lives in a meaningful way.
God made all persons equal in dignity,
And from this truth, we should no longer stray.

Humanitarians

Why not be a bridge builder,
And major highways connect?
You will make easier the travel of others;
Therefore, on society you will have an effect.

Why not be a cross bearer,
And the burdens of others help to share?
Because God has wonderfully bless you,
For the well-being of others you should care.

Why not be a torch carrier,
And for the good causes lead the way?
New ground forever remains to be broken,
You could lead us to a brighter day.

Why not be a peace maker,
And bring an end to needless strife?
There is joy in harmonious living:
So you can help to improve the quality of life.

Draw your plans for building bridges.
Prepare for the crosses which you will bear.
Light the torch then begin your march.
Assure us tranquillity and remove our fear.

Impact

Upon society are you making an impact,
Through the various endeavors which you're pursuing?
Are you finding joy in your challenging pursuits,
Or are they ordeals that you are merely enduring?
Think of your work as laying a foundation
For those who later must travel this road.
In some way are you making a contribution
To help relieve tomorrow's heavy load?
Are you seeking to develop solutions
That will the next generation serve;
That will help resolve complicated problems
And menace of society begin to unnerve?
Are you seeking to be creative,
And will leave behind you a work of art?
Will you leave some lasting reminders
That for humanity you did your part?
Will your life be an inspiration
That for others a light provide?
Will the story which you have written
Be for the doubtful a useful guide?

Upon life make an impact,
That will account for years, here, you've spent.
History, then, will record that you lived
And affected humanity to some extent.

Influencing the Future

The next generation I can influence
By the character which I display.
A role model for others I can be
And keep another from going astray.
From my mouth can come words of wisdom,
Which can for the hopeless be a useful guide.
For someone I can provide a listening ear,
And be the one in whom to confide.
For the youth an example I can set
On how with adversity I am able to cope.
Perhaps, one can learn by observation
That life can be successful when built on hope.
I can live a life that can be a lesson
For one who is seeking the right direction.
And perhaps, in years that follow,
In some youth can be seen my reflection.

The next generation I can influence
Through both my words and my deeds.
If of this I am fully aware,
Flowers will outnumber the useless weeds.

Integrity

If you build your house on integrity,
Solid will be its foundation.
Against it human storms can beat
But endure it will, in any situation.
Fear not the temptations you daily face,
Integrity is firm and will solidly stand.
Alien influences cannot undermine it
For over your actions you have command.
From faulty decisions you will be sheltered,
Since integrity for you will be a guide.
When others attempt to mislead you,
Look upon integrity as a source of pride.
When in delicate situations you are involved,
Because of integrity you can stand fast.
You will have no doubt which action to take,
For integrity will guide you as in the past.
When contrary principles try to overwhelm you,
Integrity always you must maintain.
After it sees you through the deep,
A sense of accomplishment you will obtain.
Fear not the consequences.
With integrity you cannot go wrong.
Foes you will encounter along the way,
But with integrity you can be strong.

New Life for the Nation

New life to the nation
we must bring
and revived hope

to the people give.
Courage, we must employ
in all that we do
As upon new horizon
we set our eyes.
Greater global responsibility
let us prepare to accept.
For heavy burdens of the world
someone must bear.
Our shoulders are capable
of undertaking such a task
and our minds are prepared
to offer new ideas.
To the "least of these"
we can give hope
by creative programs
we put into effect.
To those who are talented
we can encourage
by providing opportunities
for fulfillment of their dreams.
If to God
we look for guidance,
creative leadership
we will be able to assume
A master-plan for success
He will help us to design.
For the challenging new venture
on which we are embarked.

Racism

Racism is a major menace,
Which we should banish from this land.
No one should be punished because of race;
Against it we must take a stand.
Racism does harm to the nation.
Sometimes it threatens to tear it asunder.
Solutions to this evil must be found,
Or else we'll compound the existing blunder.
Racism weakens our voice abroad,
When the virtue of democracy we proclaim.
Diplomats of other countries often remind us
That we must first achieve our aim.
Racism must not be allowed to destroy us;
With all our forces we must resist this wrong.
Contagious is this growing menace,
Which in a democracy does not belong.
Do we aid the cause of racism
By the silence which we maintain?
Our voices we must raise against it.
From this struggle we cannot abstain.

Seize the Opportunity

Seize now the opportunity.
It may never come your way again.
Make use of this golden moment.
Strike now, and your goal obtain.

Very seldom is there a void;
Therefore, on the stage be ready to appear.
When opportunity beckons you,
Your act perform without a fear.

Be mindful of future events.
Of special days be fully aware.
Build your programs around them,
And you'll be regarded as very rare.
Some occasions call for courage,
Which only a few can understand.
Since your training has prepared you,
Act forcefully and take command.

Good ideas are always needed--
Suggestions that are very rare.
You, too, can be creative.
For this occasion you should prepare.
Seize now the opportunity
By standing in reserve.
Whenever the major actor falters,
Assume the role and faithfully serve.

Time to Awake

From your sleep you must awake
To pursue goals of which you dream.
Already you are far behind your schedule,
And rigorous is the task of swimming upstream.

There are many obstacles which will confront you--
Many barriers remain for you to move.
Now you must act with determination,
For there is much which we can improve.

Sleep is a time in which to dream,
But for action you must be wide awake.
If dreams are to be brought to their fruition,
Of difficult assignments you must partake.
Critical decisions already await you,
Which long ago should have been made.
Unless you are committed to serious efforts,
Your long held dreams will begin to fade.

Awake now and prove that you are worthy
Of achieving the goals for which you strive.
Demonstrate that when work is needed,
You are not lacking in the necessary drive.
Be alert to destructive critics,
Who, your goals would like to derail.
Be aware and ready for action.
Show the world that you can prevail.

The Past is With Us

The past is with us more than we think.
It cannot easily be tossed aside.
It colors the actions which we must take.
To many of us it is a source of pride.

The past is with us and will always stay.
For some of us it is all we possess.
Failures in life we can choose to forget,
While long remembering our greatest success.

See not yesterday from a distorted vision.
Misjudgment, it will cause you to make.
Assess the past for what it is worth,
For too much of value is at stake.

Mistakes of the past often haunt us,
Inflicting upon us excruciating pain.
Its scars are there as a lasting reminder.
Daily, we can feel the unnecessary strain.

About the Author

Jake C. Miller, a retired political science professor, is the author of three books, including a collection of poetry entitled *Building a Better World* (1997). In *A Century of Hope,* he perceives the beginning of the 21st Century as an appropriate time to call attention to societal problems of our day. Miller uses poetry to identify crucial issues and to suggest meaningful ways to resolve them. Considering the many technological innovations of the last years of the 20th Century, he sees this century as one of hope which could easily become one of disillusionment if adequate steps are not taken to eliminate the menaces which threaten us personally, socially and environmentally. The author challenges us to entertain visions of greatness and to work for their fulfillment. *A Century of Hope* was written to inspire readers to be innovative both in their thinking and action.

www.ingramcontent.com/pod-product-compliance
Ingram Content Group UK Ltd.
Pitfield, Milton Keynes, MK11 3LW, UK
UKHW040016200726
13854UKWH00001B/230